M E D
I C I
N A L
C H E F

The
MEDICINAL
CHEF

Anxiety &
depression

Eat your way to better health

DALE PINNOCK

CONTENTS

WHEN WE THINK OF HEALTH CRISES IN THE MODERN WORLD TODAY, WE MAY UNDERSTANDABLY THINK ABOUT RISING RATES OF CANCER, OR FRIGHTENING STATISTICS REGARDING HEART DISEASE.

Maybe the obesity epidemic springs to mind, or the accelerating numbers of newly diagnosed patients with type-2 diabetes. These are certainly some of the most unnerving, dismaying and – above all – mostly avoidable health crises in modern life. However, there is one area of our health that is declining rapidly, yet is so often not talked about and further, in many cases, is often treated with disdain, or ridicule. This is our mental health.

We are not talking the full-blown stereotypical clinical mental health breakdowns. We are talking about issues that affect large portions of the population, at a level to which they can still function, but daily life can really become a misery. Depression and anxiety have become serious issues in the modern world. Thankfully, they are becoming more widely recognised and are beginning to be taken far more seriously in primary medical care.

As little as 15–20 years ago, depression was far less an accepted long-term medical condition and patients were often treated with a 'snap-out-of-it' mentality, but, with advances in research and campaigning from sufferers and support organisations, recognition of the conditions has greatly improved. In the UK it is estimated that one in four women and one in 10 men will, at some point in their life, experience an episode of depression severe enough to warrant treatment. Most of these cases are in the mild to moderate category and most will be treated in primary care. Women, do seem to be at higher risk for depressive disorders and associated morbidity. This is thought to be as a result of a combination of factors: biological, psychological and sociocultural. Women are of course also open to depression during pregnancy and post-natally due to roller-coaster hormonal fluctuations. These will not be covered in this book, but some of the same dietary patterns are of relevance. Other risk factors for both sexes are chronic or debilitating disease (many sufferers of chronic ongoing health concerns are likely to develop depression to one level or another), family history, lifestyle and socioeconomic influences.

AN OVERVIEW OF THE PROBLEM

Anxiety is now one of the most common mental health disorders in the UK, but it is greatly under-reported, under-diagnosed and most certainly under-treated. Around 4.7 per cent of the UK population experience anxiety and around 9.7 per cent experience anxiety combined with depression! This is significant.

Seasonal Affective Disorder is another issue that is a particular blight here in the UK. It is essentially a depression that comes on in the winter. For a long time it was written off as a 'bit of the winter blues', or something that was all in the mind and wasn't taken that seriously. Now, however, we have much greater insight and the condition is recognised by physicians globally. The symptoms can be very similar to depression and can begin as early as September and last through until March! Here in the UK, unsurprisingly, we have some of the worst levels of SAD sufferers. Let's face it, for much of the year the sun is little more than a rumour!

Each of the above conditions will be explored more closely in their own sections in this book.

It is clear these issues are on the rise. Why? Well, I'd love to have all of the answers, I truly would. But I feel that it is a cumulative effect of many influences of modern life on good old planet Earth. At no other point in history have we been placed under more unrealistic pressures. We have created a situation for ourselves that is far removed from how we were supposed to live. We are facing stress at a level never before seen. Don't forget, our physiology is still the same as it has been for hundreds of thousands of years. It hasn't caught up with our rapid evolution (perhaps read that as devolution?). Our stresses used to be famine, or predators. Now we are facing insane pressures to succeed, pressures regarding how we live in comparison to others. Pressures on our finances. We are in an age of unmatched communication capacity, yet feel more isolated and alone than at any point in history. We are living in madness.

Then, of course, there is the food. That is where I come in. The food that dominates in the modern world is despicable. Can food cause depression or anxiety... well, to be honest, I have no belief that it does in and of itself. But what I do believe is this:

A) It can be a major contributing factor. Let's not forget that our brain and nervous system is an organ and tissue system that, like any other, has its own unique and specific nutritional needs. If these are not met, then the functioning of the system will be impaired.

B) I think food can be a very valid, effective, safe and affordable part of the treatment protocol. Not an alternative. I'm talking about a strong and valid part of the picture. If our brain and nervous system is adequately nourished then it will function to its best ability. It can then directly affect how we respond to different situations, how things affect us and how quickly we can bounce back.

With so many influences and pressures, it is hardly surprising that we find ourselves more challenged than ever before. Well, there is little we can do about the world outside, but our diet and lifestyle is the one area where we *can* exert some control and that is what I will aim to explore throughout this book.

ARE MIND AND BODY SEPARATE, OR DOES ONE FEED THE OTHER?

I remember many moons ago, when I was doing my access course before going off to University, two of the subjects I studied were philosophy and psychology. Almost every single lesson fascinated me but one area – that very soon spilled over into biology, too – was the age-old question as to whether 'mind' and 'body' are distinctly separate entities and facets of the human creature... or is it that one is the expression of the other? Theologians and thinkers in abundance have pondered over and debated this. Many religions and traditional viewpoints see the mind as the representation of the more spiritual dimension of our existence. In certain areas of psychology, we are just viewed as being the product of our internal biochemistry. There is even a branch of specialist healthcare called 'mind-body' medicine. The truth is, there is no hard and fast answer and that is what makes it so fascinating.

What makes a musical genius, or Albert Einstein, different from those who don't possess such talent? Are they biochemically different? No. Do they have anatomical differences in their brain? Well, sometimes, but even that is not always consistent. There is still mystery surrounding the human mind and the many things that are at the core of our nature and I, for one, am glad that mystery is there. I believe it is meant to be there. Without that mystery, life would suddenly become sterile mediocrity.

We are yet to understand what makes music move us, what causes us to fall in love, what creates our unique spark and quirks, or what gives us our little individual traits. Is it merely the total sum of our perceptions of the world, based on our own experiences, filtered through the five apertures of the senses, that are processed in accordance to other previously held beliefs arrived at in the same way? Is it just a mindless series of chemical reactions and physiological processes and changes? Or is there something else? Something more.

In recent years we have begun to understand more about the physiology of the mind, to a degree. We have started to understand neurotransmitters (these will come up again soon) and the impact that they have on mood. We are understanding more about how the neurons work, what factors affect memory and cognition. Most interesting to me, however, is the way in which something as relatively simple as nutrition can profoundly influence this. Just a small tweak in what we have for lunch and dinner can influence our mind and mood. Now that is fascinating.

The research being done in this area these days is phenomenal. Organisations such as Food and Behaviour Research are really helping to shape our understanding of how and what nutrition influences our minds (www.fabresearch.org is seriously worth a look, there is a staggering archive of research there). The implications of this really could be profound, as it seems that our mental health on a global scale is taking a nose dive, the cost to world health services is growing and the effectiveness of treatment is questionable in all but the most mild of cases. What if there were something else we could bring into the picture. Something that each of us could exercise a little bit of control over.

ANATOMY OF THE NERVOUS SYSTEM

As is a recurrent theme in my work, I feel that it is important for you to get a better understanding of how the nervous system works, what it is composed of and so on, so that you can really appreciate how the information that follows later in the book is relevant. The physiology of the nervous system is incredibly complex and things can start to get quite Byzantine when we get it down to the smallest detail. So what I have done here is taken the key important points, the ones that have the most relevance to nutritional intervention, and condensed them for you.

CENTRAL AND PERIPHERAL

The nervous system can basically be divided into two distinct sections: the central nervous system (CNS) and the peripheral. The central nervous system consists of the brain and the spinal cord. This is essentially like a control centre. It receives all the sensory information from throughout the body and can decode this and instigate the relevant responses. It also makes decisions regarding specific responses and sends that message to the relevant area of the body, via the peripheral nervous system. So, as is probably obvious, the peripheral nervous system has two jobs. Delivering sensory information to the CNS and carrying signals from the CNS to the peripheries. To give you an idea how this works: you touch something hot. The nerves in the peripheral nervous system detect this and carry the signal to your central nervous system. The central nervous system then decodes the signal and thinks 'ouch, that's hot, I need to get my hand away from that'. So, the central nervous system sends out a signal to instigate that very response. The signal goes from the CNS to the peripheral nervous system so that the correct muscles are stimulated to cause the retraction of your hand. This all happens in a fraction of a second, but highlights how the two areas are separate but work together.

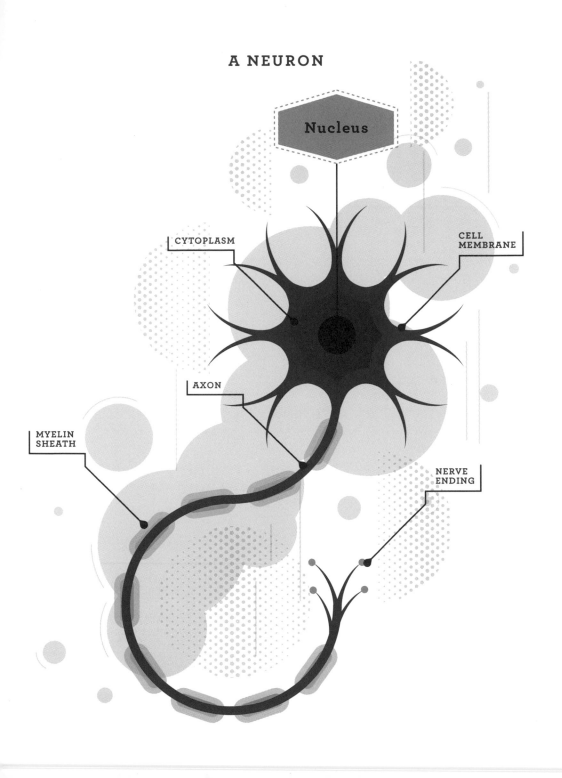

A NEURON

Nucleus

CYTOPLASM

CELL MEMBRANE

AXON

MYELIN SHEATH

NERVE ENDING

THE NEURON:
Neurons are one of the most important things to understand when it comes to any aspect of nervous system health. Their structure and function can be very profoundly affected by nutrition and even the slightest lack of key nutrients can have effects on the nervous system that may result in a profound experience for anyone affected. Let's first look at the parts of the neuron and at how each individual bit works:

AXON
The axon is essentially the long fibrous projection of a neuron. They can vary massively in length. Some can get as long as a metre, while others are as short as a millimetre.

Their function is to transmit information. This could be sensory information, as in our earlier example of touching something hot. Or it could also be information that instigates movement. Axons touch other neurons (almost), muscles and glands. They carry their signal in the form of a special electrical impulse called an action potential. This electrical impulse moves across the axon at an insanely fast pace until it reaches the axon terminal, which is the very end point of the neuron that you can see on the diagram on the previous page. For neurons that aren't directly feeding muscles or tissues, it appears that they are touching each other back to back. However there is in fact a gap between them, known as the synapse. When the action potential reaches the terminal end of the axon it has to deliver the impulse across the gap. The synapse.

SYNAPSE AND COMMUNICATION BETWEEN NEURONS
The synapse is the gap in between two neurons. As previously outlined, the signal that moves along a neuron is electrical, in the form of an action potential. This signal cannot, however, jump across the synapse. It needs to be carried across by different means. Enter the neurotransmitter.

Neurotransmitters are chemical communication molecules that take the message that is being delivered by the action potential and translate it into a chemical message that is capable of jumping the gap between neurons, where it gets translated back in to an action potential... and so it continues.

As the action potential moves along the axon and reaches the terminal, it triggers a different set of processes. At the terminal, there are small vesicles (sacs) filled with different neurotransmitters that cause different types of responses to take place. Different signals activate the vesicles containing different neurotransmitters.

These vesicles then move to the very edge of the membrane at the axon terminal and release their contents, the neurotransmitters, into the synapse. On the neighbouring neuron, there are specialised receptors that are designed to recognise specific neurotransmitters. When they recognise a specific neurotransmitter, they know what signal (in the form of an action potential) to trigger in the neuron.

So, the electrical signal gets to the end of the axon, gets translated into a chemical signal that can move across the synapse, gets picked up by a receptor, then gets translated back into an action potential again where the process continues, until the response is given. This response may be moving your arm, or trying to remember an important date. Whatever the neurological response, the same principles essentially apply.

THE MYELIN SHEATH

The myelin sheath is a very important structure indeed. It is required for proper nerve function and is designed to maximise a neuron's communication capacity. The myelin sheath is an outcropping of cell membranes that are composed of proteins and specialised fatty material.

It is there to allow the electrical impulses in neurons – the action potential – to jump across the axon rather than simply flowing across it and this makes the action potential travel like lightning.

If you look at the earlier diagram (see page 13), the myelin sheath is not a single envelope that wraps the axon, but rather is laid out as a series of little capsules along the length of the axon. Between these little capsules are tiny areas of exposed axon. These are called 'Nodes of Ranvier'. The action potential jumps from node to node, travelling across the axon quicker. Even the slightest degradation of the myelin sheath can drastically affect the functioning of the neuron and, in extreme circumstances such as multiple sclerosis where the immune system attacks the myelin sheath, the results can be devastating and life-threatening. As such, the body constantly maintains the myelin sheath and requires key building blocks to do this, which are: dietary fats!

NEUROTRANSMITTERS AND RECEPTORS

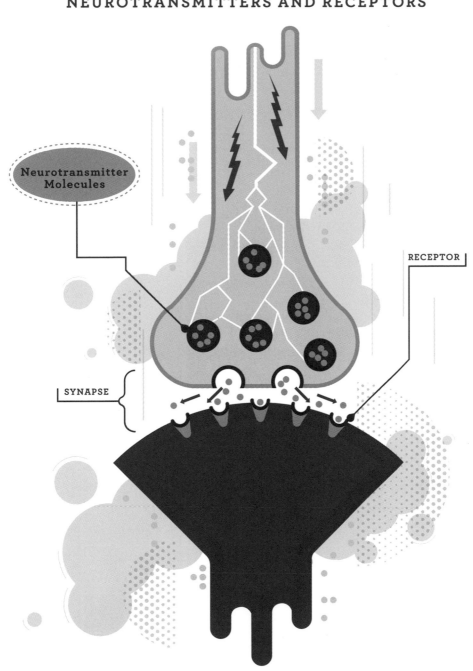

Neurotransmitter
Molecules

RECEPTOR

SYNAPSE

NEUROTRANSMITTERS: THE COMMUNICATION KEYS

As briefly outlined on the previous pages, the main signals that are carried throughout our nervous system are electrical impulses that travel along the axon at lightning speed. Neurons don't actually physically touch each other. There is a gap between them which is called the synapse. The electrical impulse isn't able to jump this gap, so another method needs to be employed in order to keep the signal moving along through the network of neurons.

Within the terminal end of the neuron there are little vesicles – small sacs – that are filled with different types of neurotransmitters. It is the job of a neurotransmitter to communicate to the neighbouring neuron what type of signal is being sent, so it knows how to respond in order to continue the chain of communication. As the signal moves along the axon, it will eventually come to the terminal end. When it gets to this end point, the relevant vesicle comes into action and begins to migrate towards the edge of the membrane of the axon. As it gets to the edge, it almost fuses with the membrane, then pushes out and breaks through the membrane wall, spilling the neurotransmitter out into the synapse (the space between neurons).

The neurotransmitter then moves along to the neighbouring neuron, where receptors that are designed to detect that specific neurotransmitter find it and then tell the inner workings of the neuron what signal is being sent and what it needs to do.

An electrical impulse then begins, travels along the neuron... and so the chain of events continues. It isn't really necessary to know all of the ins and outs of the different neurotransmitters, as things can start getting quite complex. But I do feel that a basic grasp of them is needed, as this is one of the key areas where nutrition can influence our nervous system. So I will take a quick look at the most important neurotransmitters now.

ACETYLCHOLINE

This is a neurotransmitter that wears many hats at once. It is active in both the central and peripheral nervous systems. It is involved in movement, both voluntary and involuntary. It plays both an excitatory and inhibitory role, which basically means that it can speed up and increase responses, or slow down and decrease them.

In the central nervous system it plays a vital role in memory and learning and is involved in neuroplasticity: the development of new nerve connections and pathways in the brain when we learn new things. Every time we learn something new, such as a skill or a fact, new pathways and connections between neurons take place. This change and growth is called neuroplasticity. It is an important part of arousing our senses when we wake up in the morning.

Acetylcholine is a very important part of the decision-making process. I don't mean sitting pondering over a subject such as 'shall I do that skydive?'. I'm talking about those automatic, almost unconscious decisions that we make in response to sensory stimuli. A good example of this would be the same as I gave before: when you touch something hot and pretty quickly realise that it may be a good idea to get your hand out of the way. A deficit of acetylcholine has been associated with Alzheimer's disease and depression. (There is no suggestion that reduced levels of acetylcholine is a cause, there has just been an association found. The low levels may be because of the conditions.)

SEROTONIN

Serotonin has to be the most well-known of all neurotransmitters. It is one of those things that gets widely talked about, everybody has heard of it and it has almost become a bit fashionable. I think this is because it is a neurotransmitter that is very widely understood and one that has become a key target in drug therapy for some of our most debilitating mental health issues. Why is this? Serotonin is one of the main neurotransmitters that is involved in how we feel.

It is synthesised in the body from the amino acid tryptophan and over 90 per cent of it is stored in the gut! It has many roles to play in the body, from controlling elements of bone metabolism, to controlling localised aspects of gut function. However, the one thing that serotonin does that really overshadows everything else, is make us feel good!

Serotonin is the feel-good chemical that keeps us happy and upbeat. It keeps mood stable, too. Serotonin regulates our appetite, regulates sleep patterns, is involved in memory and sexual desire. A deficiency of serotonin has been linked to depression, while serotonin levels and its availability in the nervous system is a major target in drug therapy for depression.

GABA

GABA – gamma amino butyric acid – is another neurotransmitter that is greatly involved with how we feel. It reduces anxiety and stress and regulates epinephrine and norepinephrine (see below and right), dopamine and serotonin (see right and above). This neurotransmitter is vital in mood regulation.

EPINEPHRINE

Epinephrine, otherwise known as adrenaline, is both a hormone and a neurotransmitter. This is the stuff that we get a surge of during the stress response. When we experience emotions such as fear or anger, adrenaline is released in order to allow us to respond to the situation: to fight or take flight. It acts to increase heart rate, increase blood pressure, increase muscle strength and speed up sugar metabolism. In essence, it can divert blood to necessary tissues and increase energy metabolism in times of stress to give our body the necessary capacity to respond to the stressful stimuli, run for our lives or stand up and fight. Low levels in the body can lead to fatigue and lack of focus, while excess has been linked with ADHD, disturbed sleep patterns, anxiety and excitability.

NOREPINEPHRINE

Norepinephrine is closely related to epinephrine and is also released from the adrenal glands. It is involved in increasing blood pressure by causing constriction of blood vessels. It also enhances mental focus and concentration and, like epinephrine, it increases the circulation of free fatty acids to increase the available fuel for tissues to metabolise during the stress response. These are important elements of the stress response, as they help us to escape or manage stressful situations.

DOPAMINE

Dopamine is one of the most talked about neurotransmitters in the press, especially when discussing matters of addiction. It is a neurotransmitter that really is central to our motivation, drive and interest in life.

It can also be viewed as a neurotransmitter involved in stress, but stress of a positive nature, such as falling in love, exercising, having sex and so on. It is the neurotransmitter that plays a role in addiction, as it is involved in alerting us to a potential reward; if a person is an alcoholic, then the sight or thought of a drink will cause an increase in dopamine activity in certain areas in the brain and we get the sense that a reward is coming.

But dopamine is also involved in slightly less shady things, such as movement and mental focus. Low levels of dopamine at the extreme level can result in Parkinson's disease, where neurons that produce dopamine begin to die off. Low-level deficiency can lead to lack of motivation, fatigue and poor concentration.

GLUTAMATE

Glutamate is the king of excitatory neurotransmitters, meaning it stimulates and gets things going. It is a very important aspect of learning and memory function. Its amino acid precursor, glutamine (often used in sports supplements and by bodybuilders and so on),

"If you don't think your anxiety, depression, sadness and stress impact your physical health, think again. All of these emotions trigger chemical reactions in your body, which can lead to inflammation and a weakened immune system."

KRIS CARR

used to be a prominent feature in the barrage of 'brain food' type supplements that were popular a few years ago. However, there had been questions over its safety and its potential to be an excitotoxin. I personally think a little can be very beneficial. The balance of glutamate in the brain is a very finite one. It is vital for learning and memory but excessive amounts are associated with neuronal dysfunction, while changes in glutamine levels are part of the pathological picture in issues such as Alzheimer's, Parkinson's and Tourette's. This fine balance is essential.

PEA

Phenylethylamine, or PEA for short, is something of a special substance and one that has become a bit of a darling of the health world. Understandably so, really. PEA is a compound that is released when we fall in love. Basically it speeds up the to and fro of information between neurons. Just the smallest amount of it can induce feelings of euphoria, bliss, infatuation and love. While it is produced in the brain, it is also present in some foods, including... chocolate! This may explain a lot... Low levels of PEA have been associated with depression.

KEY NUTRIENTS IN MENTAL HEALTH

OMEGA 3

The human brain is almost 60 per cent fat. That isn't purely by chance, or that the brain happens to be a convenient place for fat to be dumped. This fat is completely functional and has a vital role to play. The fatty element of our brain needs constant maintenance as it is susceptible to damage from normal metabolic processes and must be constantly replaced and rebuilt.

In order to carry out this continual maintenance, the body needs an adequate supply of the right types of fats. This is where things can start to go a little pear-shaped in the modern world. Our fat intake has really changed and for the worse. Now, I'm not going to start talking about saturated fats and all that. Quite the opposite in fact. The fear of saturated fat is what caused the problem.

It all started in the late 1950s, via an American physiologist by the name of Ancel Keys. He had started to develop a hypothesis that saturated fat intake was associated with heart disease, and he set out to prove it. Keys developed a study of 22 countries which, as you might suppose, set out to study the diets of 22 countries and compare these diets with incidence of heart disease. When Keys published his findings, the results were unequivocal. They showed a beautiful curve and the association between saturated fat intake and heart disease was very strong. However... the study was published as 'The Seven Countries Study'. The results given were from just seven of the 22 countries. The seven countries whose data supported this hypothesis. Had the results of all 22 countries been published there would have been *no association* whatsoever shown.

But, alas, this study was taken as a revelation and, very shortly afterwards, massive public health campaigns began in the USA and very quickly followed to the UK. These campaigns set out to warn us of the dangers of saturated fat and encourage us instead to opt for 'heart-healthy' fats such as vegetable oils and margarines.

What's wrong with this, you may ask? Well, these oils contain a very high proportion of fatty acids known as omega 6 fatty acids. Now, these *are* essential fatty acids, meaning our body can't manufacture them and needs to get them from the diet. The problem is, we only need a very small amount of them, any excess beyond the level we need gets metabolised in a different way to form compounds that can stimulate and worsen inflammation.

The drastic shift in dietary fat intake in the last decades has meant that in the UK we take in almost 23 times more omega 6 fatty acids than we need *per day*! The important point here is, if we are consuming that much omega 6, then we won't be consuming any where near enough omega 3: the most vital fats that the brain needs. Add to this the fact that omega 3 and omega 6 are both processed by the same systems. The more 6 is there, the more competition there is with 3 for the systems that process them. So, our intake of these fats really needs reviewing and I would encourage everyone to reduce their intake of omega 6 and increase their omega 3 intake, not just for the health of the brain, but also for many other aspects of health, especially that of the cardiovascular system (see my book *Heart disease: Eat your way to better health*, for a deeper insight into this). To give you an idea of the importance of omega 3 fatty acids in the brain, let's take a look at the two main functional omega 3 fatty acids: EPA and DHA.

EPA
Eicosapentaenoic acid, or EPA for short, is one of the most highly active of the omega 3 family. There are three forms of omega 3: ALA (often found in seeds such as flax and chia); EPA; and DHA (both found in oily fish). In theory, the plant form ALA is the precursor in humans for EPA, as a series of enzymes and processes changes ALA into EPA. However, in actuality, humans are incredibly poor at this conversion, with an average rate of about 10–15 per cent, apart from pregnant women who can ramp it up another 10–15 per cent.

So, to really get the benefits and sufficient intake to deliver them, it is best that we take EPA in a way that is already pre-formed: eating plenty of oily fish and, of course, looking at supplements.

There have been hundreds and hundreds of studies that have shown that increased EPA intake improves many aspects of brain health and function and benefits many conditions, from the mild to the serious.

One interesting thing about EPA is that it has been found to protect the vital phospholipids in the brain from breakdown by an enzyme called phospholipase, which naturally works to liberate fatty acids from cell membranes. The phospholipids are the important complex fatty substances that make up the membranes of cells, including neurons. They need to be able to function at their best in order to allow the flow of information across them and on to other cells. In protecting the phospholipids in such a way, EPA helps to keep the phospholipid bilayer (cell membrane) in better shape, ensuring it is able to work at its best. There is also a chain of thought, still developing through research, that EPA can enhance both membrane fluidity and the performance of neurotransmitter receptors and therefore also have a degree of influence upon neurotransmitter release.

There is another influence that omega 3 has that may have a part to play in its positive effect upon the health of the brain. That is the regulation of inflammation. There have been links arising between chronic inflammation and depression, for example. The fatty acids in our diet are metabolised to form some quite powerful communication compounds. Among these are a group of compounds called prostaglandins, which regulate the inflammatory response. There are three main types of prostaglandin: Series 1, Series 2 and Series 3. Series 1 has mild anti-inflammatory activity. Series 2 is a powerful stimulant and activator of inflammation. Series 3, on the other hand, is a very powerful anti-inflammatory. Different dietary fatty acids are metabolised to form different types of prostaglandins. If, for example, our intake of dietary fats is predominantly of omega 6, then we will start to make far higher amounts of the pro-inflammatory Series 2 prostaglandins that can cause chronic inflammation, or drastically fan the flame of any inflammation already present. On the other hand, if we consume more omega 3, especially in the EPA form, we will force our body to produce far higher amounts of the anti-inflammatory Series 3 prostaglandins, which will notably reduce inflammation.

The question is, whether there is any direct localised inflammatory activity occurring in the nervous system that may have a causative effect upon certain conditions and issues, or whether there is another factor associated with inflammation that is having an effect. Whatever the circumstance, the approach of reducing omega 6 and increasing omega 3 will deliver numerous health benefits to numerous body systems and is one of my top tips for better nutrition.

DHA

The other vitally important omega 3 fatty acid: docosahexaenoic acid. This has different roles to play in the brain at different stages of life. During pregnancy and early infant development, DHA is vital for the growth of neurons and other brain structures. These tissues are constantly developing and changing at a rapid speed and DHA is needed constantly.

DHA is equally as important for adult brains too, but for different reasons. Firstly, it is an important component of the phospholipids in the brain, the fatty substances that make up cell membranes and whose optimal health equate to optimal functioning. DHA can make the phospholipid bilayer (cell membrane) more fluid. In doing so, it helps to improve cell function and signalling and the exchange of data across cell membranes. DHA is vital for the consistent formation of new nerve connections and ongoing regulation of neuron structure.

"One cannot think well,
love well, sleep well,
if one has not dined well."

VIRGINIA WOOLF

It is also an important structural material for the health of the myelin sheath and neurotransmitter receptors, both of which can be susceptible to damage. Maintaining their structure is vital, which the body can do quite easily with the right components. DHA also plays a very important part in cell signalling both inside and outside of cells. DHA also produces two relatively newly discovered compounds that help to protect the cells in the brain and nervous system. These are called resolvins and protectins. Their names give you a hint as to what they do. Resolvins resolve inflammatory episodes in the brain. This doesn't refer to acute inflammation such as you would see in meningitis or trauma, but more the low-grade chronic inflammation that can lead to changes and long-term damage within the brain. Protectins, well, they protect the brain from potential damage from inflammatory episodes.

Best food sources of EPA and DHA:

Anchovies
Herrings
Mackerel
Salmon
Spirulina (DHA)

ARACHIDONIC ACID

This is another fatty acid that is seldom talked about and, when it is, it is only usually its negative attributes that get covered. It is one of those substances that can deliver both health-giving and damaging effects when the balance gets out of kilter. It is found in red meats, egg yolks and offal and is in the omega 6 family of fatty acids. I always recommend that people reduce their intake of these fatty acids from vegetable oils and the like and I stand firmly by this recommendation. However, a small amount from natural sources is very important (we just need to ensure that overall our intake of omega 3 far outweighs our intake of omega 6).

Arachidonic acid plays some profoundly important roles in the brain and is actually one of the most abundant fatty acids there. Arachidonic acid helps maintain membrane fluidity in the hippocampus area of the brain, which is involved in memory and spatial awareness. It also helps to protect neurons from oxidative stress and activates a protein called syntaxin-3 which repairs neurons. As I have stressed, too much of the omega 6 fatty acids, in particular arachidonic acid, can actually trigger and exacerbate inflammation. So, rather than taking supplements of omega 6 as so many people unwisely do, I'd just rely on good cuts of meat and a scattering of nuts and seeds in your diet to cover your bases.

Best food sources of arachidonic acid:

Good-quality red meats
Nuts
Offal
Seeds

B VITAMINS

These are a group of nutrients with very far-reaching functions that carry out vital roles in virtually every conceivable tissue and body system. This means that, when consumed, they are very widely distributed throughout the body. Unfortunately, many of us eating a modern diet are consuming very little of them. Combine these two factors with the fact that they are water soluble (so readily excreted from the body after a given period of time) and you begin to understand how it is quite easy to start getting deficient in them. This isn't good for overall health, but certainly spells trouble for our mind and brain, as they have very important roles to play there.

VITAMIN B1 (THIAMINE)

B1 is involved in turning glucose into energy. Low levels of this nutrient can lead us to feel tired and sluggish. It can also make us mentally tired and affect concentration and mental performance. Adequate energy production is essential for quick, sharp thinking.

Best food sources of B1:

Greens
Oily fish
Pork
Squash
Sunflower seeds
Whole grains

VITAMIN B3 (NIACIN)

Vitamin B3 has a long-standing association with mental health since its deficiency illness, pellagra, was understood. Sufferers of pellagra get a thick scaly skin rash on exposure to sunlight, but they also suffer from depression, disorientation and apathy. Since that discovery, niacin has also been used in several studies of the treatment of schizophrenia, and has also shown promise in improving the memory in both young and old people.

Best food sources of B3:

Brown rice
Chicken
Mushrooms
Prawns
Salmon
Tuna

VITAMIN B5 (PANTOTHENIC ACID)

Vitamin B5 has a very important role to play in the brain. It is needed to make the neurotransmitter acetylcholine, which is important for memory and learning.

Best food sources of B5:

Broccoli
Eggs
Liver
Mushrooms
Squash
Sunflower seeds

VITAMIN B6 (PYRIDOXINE)

Vitamin B6 is an incredibly important nutrient for mental health. This is for two distinct reasons. Firstly, it is a key nutrient involved in the formation of myelin, that super-conductive sheath that carries signals rapidly across the axon. Secondly, it is an important nutrient for converting the amino acid tryptophan into the neurotransmitter serotonin: the feel-good compound. This neurotransmitter is a frequent target for antidepressant medication and even *slightly* low levels of it can have a profound effect upon the way that we feel.

Best food sources of B6:

Bananas
Spinach
Sunflower seeds
Sweet potato
Tuna
Turkey

FOLIC ACID

Folic acid is a B vitamin that is most commonly associated with pregnancy, but there are links with folic acid deficiency and mental health issues such as depression, too. Several studies have shown this link and there is a chain of thought that low folic acid levels lead to low levels of a substance called SAMe (s adenosylmethionine) that is involved in neurotransmitter production.

Best food sources of folic acid:

Broccoli
Kale
Lentils
Beans
Spinach

VITAMIN B12

Vitamin B12 is also showing some potential links to mental health, although the reasons behind this are slightly less clear than with other B vitamins. There are certainly associations arising from research but, in terms of establishing exact causal factors, we aren't there yet. One theory is that B12 is involved in the production of a type of neurotransmitter called monoamines, involved in emotion, cognition and arousal. It is also thought that, in combination with vitamin B6 and folic acid, B12 can reduce levels of an amino acid called homocysteine, which can cause damage to the brain and cardiovascular system.

Best food sources of B12:

Eggs
Liver

Red meat
Salmon
Shellfish

MAGNESIUM

The mineral magnesium is one of the most under-appreciated nutrients in our diets. Yet it is involved in more than 1,000 biochemical processes in the body, so its relevance to mental health is inevitable. I feel magnesium really comes up trumps in issues such as anxiety and nervous tension. This is because, firstly, it can physically relax the muscles. If you are feeling anxious, your muscles will begin to get tense and taught. Magnesium helps the muscle fibres to relax, easing the feeling of tension. Magnesium also relaxes the nervous system and plays an important role in nerve conduction.

Best food sources of magnesium:

Cashew nuts
Leafy greens
Pumpkin seeds
Quinoa

GLUTAMINE

Glutamine is an amino acid that is freely available in supplement form and is popular among body builders and athletes, due to its role in muscle maintenance. Glutamine is also the precursor to the neurotransmitter glutamate, which is a stimulating substance that can literally 'fire up' the brain. I find it especially useful to use it in supplement form before I have to really put my brain in gear, for a media interview perhaps, or anything that will require some problem-solving skills.

Best food sources of glutamine:

Beef
Dairy products
Eggs
Red cabbage

TRYPTOPHAN

Tryptophan is another amino acid of great importance to mental health. It is the precursor to the mothership of neurotransmitters: serotonin. Given the right circumstances, tryptophan will cross the blood brain barrier and get converted over into serotonin. To get tryptophan across the blood brain barrier to where it is needed, we need to consume it with a good-quality carbohydrate source. This gentle rise in insulin will allow it to get across. Tryptophan-rich foods are great for lifting mood and are especially useful for a good night's sleep, as a rise in serotonin in the evening can convert into something called melatonin, which promotes deep healthy sleep.

Best food sources of tryptophan:

Bananas
Cheese
Eggs
Tuna
Turkey

THE IMPORTANCE OF BLOOD SUGAR BALANCE

Another nutritional aspect of mental health that is very often overlooked is blood sugar management. It is a simple skill to master really, but the impact that it can have on your mind and mood is quite staggering. Basically different foods, because of their composition, will release their energy at different rates. Pure glucose, for example, will send blood sugar up very rapidly and vigorously. Glucose is actually the benchmark against which all other foods are measured. It is the simplest form of sugar, so requires no digestive effort. It goes straight into circulation. Foods vary in their make up and complexity and certain factors will influence how rapidly foods release their energy.

Fibre is one of the biggest factors. Let's compare white and brown bread, for example. Proper brown bread has all the fibre from the wheat husk and many brown breads have additional seeds and fibres added as well. White bread, on the other hand, has had all of the husks removed and the fibre content is drastically lower. The fibre in the brown bread will simply make the sugars in the bread harder to get to and will require more digestive effort to release them. With the refined white bread, on the other hand, the lack of fibre makes the sugar much easier to get at. In the higher fibre food, the sugar is released at a slower, steady pace, whereas with refined foods it is released at a very rapid pace as it takes far less digestive effort to liberate the glucose.

Another influence on this are the combinations in which you eat certain foods. Adding protein to your carbohydrates for example will require a great deal more digestive effort to liberate the glucose, as proteins are digested more slowly so there is a lot more work for the digestive system to do when you have a combination of protein and carbohydrate. The result is a slow even drip-feeding of glucose into the bloodstream rather than a giant surge.

Why does any of this matter? Because, if you consume foods that flood your bloodstream with sugar, the initial feeling is rather pleasant. You get a high. But this barrage of sugar is no good for us at all and the body has very fast-acting, responsive ways of dealing with it. When it occurs, we rapidly secrete insulin. This hormone tells our cells to take in glucose as quickly as possible and put it to good use. If blood sugar stays that high for long it can cause damage. The problem is, when this happens, our blood sugar plummets and we get a sugar dip. This makes us feel tired, groggy, irritable and can make our moods spiral downwards. This is why balance is important. While the physiology and so on may seem a tad complex, putting all of it into practice is rather straightforward. Here are the golden rules:

GO WHOLESOME:
It's time to ditch the white refined grain products. White bread, white rice, white pasta: in the bin! Instead move over to whole grain versions. These have their fibre intact, so will be harder to digest and will release their sugars slowly. It is also worth bringing your overall intake down a little; we are all eating a few too many carbs.

FOOD COMBINE:
Making better choices in terms of the carbohydrates that we eat is one part of the picture. The other part is how you compose your meals. Always aim to have a good-quality carbohydrate with a good source of protein. So, chicken with quinoa, scrambled eggs on toast, fish with vegetables and sweet potato wedges. You get the picture. By having a good source of protein, you slow down the release of the sugars from the meal, giving blood sugar a nice slow consistent drip-feeding, rather than carpet-bombing it.

See? Nice and simple. The recipes in this book release their energy slowly and are composed in clever combinations, with all the key nutrients, too.

CONDITIONS

I'd like to take a moment now to explore the role that nutrition has to play in some of the more common mental health woes that affect a great number of the population. Can I emphasise my choice of words: 'the role that nutrition has to play'? I believe and stand by the fact that nutrition is a very powerful part of the healthcare picture. Diet can be a very effective therapeutic tool in its own right. The food that we eat directly influences the internal biochemical terrain of our body. Nutrition can, in many ways, be seen as medicinal. A drug, after all, delivers its effects by influencing the internal biochemical happenings within our body. So, with that in mind, to dismiss nutrition within the healthcare picture is at best irresponsible, at worst insane.

However, nowadays we have the opposite problem, too. There are many that will completely dismiss any kind of modern medical practice and swear blind that broccoli will save our souls. They feel that no matter what is going on, diet will be the answer. Having studied this at undergraduate and postgraduate level now, I would really truly love this to be the case. But it is not.

Diet doesn't have all of the answers all of the time. But, in virtually every circumstance, diet will have an influence. It is this fact that I build my work around. I want to show you the real picture, whether it is bright and hopeful, or somewhat bleak. Then I want to show you how best to apply that information to real life. So, with that in mind, let's look at the biggest general mental health concerns that affect us today and examine where diet fits into the equation.

ANXIETY

Anxiety is alarmingly common. It is in fact one of the most common mental health disorders in the UK, but is one that is under-reported, certainly under-diagnosed and often very ineffectively treated. It is estimated that around 4.7 per cent of the UK population experience anxiety and around 9.7 per cent experience anxiety combined with depression! This is really quite a shocking picture but, with the madness that is modern life, also unsurprising. Generalised anxiety disorder, while affecting five per cent of the population, actually accounts for almost 30 per cent of the mental issues seen by GPs. It is an issue where, in most cases, the sufferer still feels relatively in control and is conscious of the problem, so taking themselves along to their GP is more common than would be with other more serious mental health concerns. A strange observation is that anxiety does seem to affect more women than men. It is also noted that people in the 35–59 age group report the greatest levels of anxiety among adults, whereas individuals in the 16–24 age range report more anxiety than adults overall. Anxiety is often reported by specific demographics: people facing unemployment, lower incomes and those belonging to ethnic minorities all seem to have increased anxiety. A 2014 survey conducted by YouGov found that almost one in five feel anxious all of the time or a lot of the time. Only one in 20 of the survey respondents reported never feeling anxious!

Anxiety is something that really is quite natural and normal and is an important part of our survival instincts. Having an anxiety about a situation can heighten awareness, command greater thought and personal application and, of course, enable us to decide when is a good time to say no, or to turn tail and run. This is normal and something that we all experience from time to time. However, when it moves past normal healthy anxiety about genuinely intimidating situations, it becomes a problem that can in some cases become quite debilitating. This is when we move into the realms of generalised anxiety disorder!

"What we eat and drink affects not only our physical well being, but our mental state. I always say 'mind over matter is matter undermined'."

DR MOSARAF ALI

Generalised anxiety disorder is a long-term chronic issue. Instead of the odd bit of anxiety prior to a potentially problematic situation, sufferers find themselves almost consistently in an anxious state. Very often this anxiety is continuous regardless of the situation. Many sufferers report having constant anxiety. They will develop anxiety about a specific issue then, as soon as that issue is resolved or moves on, the anxiety will shift to something else.

It is a condition that offers virtually no respite as the anxiety isn't attached to a specific situation or event. It just rolls along from one life circumstance, then to the next, then to the next... The anxiety experience can manifest itself in a wide range of ways. It can be as simple as the mind racing and going over and over worries. There can also be very strong physical symptoms such as rapid heart beat, palpitations, nausea, sweating, dry mouth, chest pain and rapid shallow breathing.

HOW ANXIETY WORKS

The anxiety response, as I have said, is really something very normal and necessary. When we perceive a threat or a situation that is potentially harmful or problematic, the physiological workings of our body respond very quickly. A small gland at the very base of our brain, called the pituitary gland, is the first thing to get involved. When the signal of perceived threat comes from the brain, the pituitary springs into action and secretes a number of signalling hormones. These hormones fly through our bloodstream and get to the adrenal glands that sit above our kidneys. The adrenal glands pump out adrenaline which makes the heart pump faster, our breathing quicker, our muscles become tense and our minds become focused on the potential hazard. This all happens at lightning speed and our only perception of it is when we are right in the middle of it.

NUTRITIONAL APPROACH FOR MANAGING ANXIETY

OMEGA 3

Omega 3 fatty acids, as we have seen, are vital for the overall health of the brain. I personally would advise anybody that has issues or worries about the health of their brain and nervous system to increase their intake of omega 3. There can only be benefit.

But, what does the evidence say? Well, there is some evidence that omega 3 may offer some benefit to anxiety sufferers. A 2011 12-week double-blind cross-over trial of 68 medical students showed that omega 3 supplementation caused a significant 20 per cent reduction in anxiety, which is believed to be the first double-blind trial to suggest that omega 3 may have some anxiolytic (anxiety-reducing) benefit ①. While this study is encouraging, it is important to note that all of the participants were healthy; none had actually received a diagnosis of generalised anxiety syndrome. Would omega 3 have the same effects in patients with generalised anxiety? Well, that remains to be seen.

But there are literally hundreds of anecdotal reports of omega 3 offering benefits to patients with anxiety issues. Reports abound from practitioners, on patient forums and so on. In my opinion, I feel there is valid argument for the addition of extra omega 3 in the diet. From the very grass roots level, it is such a vital nutrient for the overall health and general functioning of the nervous system that any improved intake will equate to a general improvement to the health of these tissues. This can only offer benefit. Personally I am not scared of anecdotal evidence, as long as it is not used as a means to determine absolute fact. In light of the level of anecdotal reports regarding omega 3 and anxiety, coupled with the lack of potential harm, this furthers my conviction. Then finally, we have this early research that indicates that omega 3 can certainly deliver some level of anxiolytic activity. Put it all together and I believe there are good grounds for taking in more.

MAGNESIUM

Magnesium is one of the most deficient minerals in the modern diet but is one of the single most important nutrients, involved in more than 1,000 biochemical reactions and vital for every body system.

It also has quite the track record in the management of anxiety. The first way in which magnesium can be of benefit is by making us feel physically relaxed. When we get anxious, our muscles will naturally begin to tense and tighten.

Calcium and magnesium are the two minerals that regulate muscle contractions. When calcium floods into muscle cells, it causes muscles to contract. When magnesium floods into muscle cells, it causes muscle fibres to relax. So, by consuming magnesium during times of tension, we can encourage muscular relaxation. Magnesium also calms nervous tension and relaxes the mind. The mechanisms behind this are not clear, and little exists in terms of clinical trials. What we do have available, though, is an abundance of clinical and personal anecdote.

GLUTAMINE/GABA

One of the biggest keys in controlling anxiety is to manage the neurotransmitter GABA. This is a very powerfully inhibitory neurotransmitter. This means that it calms nervous responses rather than overly stimulates.

One thing that GABA is known to do is reduce something called beta waves in the brain. These are a type of brain wave that are associated with analytical thinking, focus and logic. In people with anxiety, beta waves are said to be 'splayed'. This means that they are heightened or exaggerated. So anything that we can do to bring this down and under control will make a massive difference to levels of anxiety. GABA isn't found in foods, but the nutrients involved in producing it are. One of the main nutrients is the amino acid glutamine. Almonds, bananas, broccoli, brown rice, lentils, oats, spinach and walnuts are all good sources of this nutrient.

BLOOD SUGAR MANAGEMENT

I have mentioned blood sugar balance earlier. But I really want to drive home the importance of this relatively simple thing and reiterate what a profound impact it can have on our physiology.

Sadly, today, we eat way too much sugar and refined carbs. This isn't just in the obvious things such as chocolate and fizzy drinks. It includes things such as white bread, white rice, white pasta and so on. Processed, refined and very nasty. As we have seen, the problem with these foods is that they require very little digestive effort to liberate their sugar. This means they can send blood sugar up very quickly, which initially makes us feel bright and energised. But sugar getting too high too quickly is extremely dangerous, so our body has a very effective way of coping with it: the hormone insulin. Insulin tells our cells to take up excess sugar as rapidly as possible. When this happens, our blood sugar plummets again.

This is where the problem starts for sufferers of anxiety. When blood sugar dips down quickly, we release the hormone adrenaline to stimulate the release of stored glucose. The problem here is that adrenaline is to anxiety what petrol is to a bonfire. It can cause rapid heartbeat, quickening of breath and a racing mind. Just what you need if you are prone to anxiety! So, as outlined earlier, the keys to keeping blood sugar stable are in reducing your overall carb intake and, when you do eat them, choosing carbs that are unrefined and whole (such as brown rice instead of white).

Another part of the picture is food combining: always making sure you have a good-quality protein with your unrefined carbs so you create a meal that takes longer to digest and therefore delivers its energy in more of a drip-feeding fashion as opposed to a carpet-bomb! Aside from avoiding the peaks and troughs that could lead to adrenaline surges, eating in such a way will also keep your overall mood more stable. This in itself can take the edge off anxiety. We are less likely to feel anxious if we are generally feeling more stable and even in our energy levels and overall mood.

NUTRITIONAL NUGGETS
TO AID ANXIETY:

Eat plenty of oily fish such as salmon, mackerel and herrings to get plenty of pre-formed omega 3.

Fill up on green leafy vegetables, as these are some of the best sources of magnesium on the planet.

Snack on nuts and seeds to provide some omega 3, magnesium and some protein to balance blood sugar.

Always eat good-quality proteins with good-quality carbs to create a meal that will digest and release its energy slowly and drip-feed your blood sugar, keeping it nice and even.

Consider a magnesium supplement of around 1,000mg daily.

DEPRESSION

The statistics for depression in the UK are... well... a depressing read. The current estimate is that one in five adults in the UK will be affected by depression at some point, with the highest number being in the 50–54 age group. Out of these, more are women. It is a condition that – frighteningly – is beginning to affect younger people, too, with 19 per cent of the over-16s in this country having reported depression to their GP. Certain demographics do appear to be at greater risk than others. A sizeable 27 per cent of people who are divorced or separated show signs of the condition, compared to 16 per cent of those that are married. Other groups such as those on a low income or the unemployed also show greater patterns of depression. The thing is, depression can be a really tricky condition, as the feelings that we can get are a normal (if occasional) part of the human experience, so often, in the early stages at least, it is difficult for the sufferer and those around them to determine normal highs and lows from depression of a more serious nature.

So, what is depression in the clinical sense? The symptoms can vary from individual to individual but common features of depression are a lasting feeling of sadness and hopelessness. There may also be a loss of interest in the things that you would usually enjoy doing, from hobbies through to social situations and interpersonal pleasures. Tearfulness can also be a frequent problem. The symptoms aren't purely mental, either; depression very often has strong physical symptoms associated with it. Severe fatigue, disturbed sleep, appetite loss or extreme appetite increase, aches and pains are all associated with depression. These symptoms can manifest themselves in many combinations from individual to individual. In its less serious incarnation, depression may leave the sufferer feeling just a little down and demotivated with life. However, when things get serious, this condition really can of being suicidal and feelings of immense hopelessness. Certain neurological conditions such as Parkinson's disease affect specific regions of the brain. Depression seems to affect multiple regions such as the prefrontal cortex, hippocampus, amygdala and thalamus. We are still in the very early days when it comes to determining the precise pathophysiology of depression, but one thing that *is* clear is that there is a series of abnormalities in the production of transmitters and their ability to instigate their relevant responses.

NUTRITIONAL APPROACH FOR MANAGING DEPRESSION

OMEGA 3 FATTY ACIDS

The link between omega 3 fatty acids and brain health has been known for a very long time. That age-old wive's tale that 'fish is good for your brains' came from somewhere and now we really are starting to see that this tale has validity. I'm sorry to break this to you, but you are a fat head! Your brain is 60 per cent fat and the fats of which it is composed play a vital role in its normal healthy functioning. One of the most important types of fat in the brain are the omega 3 fatty acids....

OMEGA 3 HELPS MAINTAIN MEMBRANES

The membranes of our neurons are vital to their performance. The membranes are composed of what is called a phospholipid bilayer, two layers of complex fatty structures that lay back to back. The healthy functioning of the membrane is essential for several reasons, all of which involve the movement of things across the membrane. As we have discussed earlier, signals move across neurons initially in the form of electrical impulses. This impulse happens in the form of charged particles moving to and fro across the membrane in a spinning, spiralling fashion. Then, as we know, the membrane in a spinning, spiralling fashion. Then, as we know, this electrical impulse reaches the very end of the neuron and can't jump across the synaptic gap, so the signal has to stimulate the release of the relevant neurotransmitter to carry on the chain of events. This consists of the vesicle, the small sac filled with neurotransmitters, moving to the edge of the membrane, fusing with the membrane, then splitting and releasing the neurotransmitter into the synaptic gap. Both of these aspects of sending signals throughout the nervous system are absolutely, completely reliant upon a healthy membrane. The fats that we eat will determine the state of our membranes, as they are the structural material that our body uses to make membranes.

But, obviously, the materials that the body has available are the materials that it uses to build membranes. If we are consuming high amounts of trans fats and excessive saturated fats (not that saturated fats are bad, it's all about ratios) and not enough of the omega 3 fatty acids, then our membranes will be stiffer, less fluid and not very responsive, while communication across them will be greatly affected. On the other hand, with sufficient intake of the right fats, such as omega 3 fatty acids, our membranes will be far more fluid and function much better and, as a result, the kinds of communication mentioned will be much more efficient. Electrical impulses will flow faster and neurotransmitters will be released more efficiently and at a higher level.

OMEGA 3 HELPS ENHANCE RECEPTOR FUNCTION

So we have seen that a healthy membrane is absolutely vital for neurons to be able to carry their signals effectively and how fatty acids play a vital role in this. The next part of the picture, once the electrical impulse has travelled along the neuron, then stimulated the release of the relevant neurotransmitter, is how the neighbouring neuron receives this signal in order to continue the flow of communication. This is where receptors come in. Receptors

Their job is to identify specific compounds, then bind to them. When a compound (technically a 'ligand') is identified, the receptor will bind to it. When it binds to it, as the receptor is built into the membrane and half of it is inside the cell, it will send signals to the inner cell and instigate specific changes or chains of events. Omega 3 fatty acids can help receptors function more effectively, partially because they help the membrane to work better, which does have a bearing on the extent to which a receptor can successfully deliver its message. Omega 3 fatty acids also seem to improve receptor function across a broad spectrum of different receptors.

OMEGA 3 REDUCES INFLAMMATION

One final area where omega 3 fatty acids may offer benefit is their impact upon inflammation. There is a growing body of research showing an association between depression and pro-inflammatory compounds. One of the key roles of fatty acids in the body is their metabolism into prostaglandins which, among other things, regulate the inflammatory response. There are three different types of prostaglandin. These are called Series 1, Series 2 and Series 3. Series 1 is mildly anti-inflammatory; Series 2 is powerfully pro-inflammatory; while Series 3 is powerfully anti-inflammatory. Different dietary fatty acids are metabolised to produce different prostaglandins. Omega 3 fatty acids tend to metabolise into anti-inflammatory prostaglandins. The omega 3 fatty acid EPA gets converted into powerfully anti-inflammatory Series 3 prostaglandin. So, the potentially anti-inflammatory action of omega 3 fatty acids may offer an extra benefit.

WHAT THE EVIDENCE TELLS US

We have a good idea as to what omega 3 fatty acids do within the brain, so in theory we could give biological plausibility to the reports that omega 3 fatty acids help symptoms of depression. But what does the evidence say? Well, this is where things get exciting.

There has been considerable epidemiological (the study of disease patterns among populations) data that shows a negative association between fish consumption and depression. A negative association basically means, in this case: the higher the fish intake, the lower the incidence of depression. For example, a study of around 4,000 Finnish nationals showed that the higher the fish consumption, the lower the risk of depression and suicidal tendencies [1]. Combined data from the 1996/97 New Zealand Health Survey and 1997 Nutrition Survey found that fish consumption was significantly associated with higher self-reported mental health status (an individual's personal perception of their mood, outlook and depression scores) [2].

Epidemiological data is interesting, as it shows patterns of association. However, these associations may be related to many other factors, so don't necessarily prove cause and effect (for example, that omega 3 was the beneficial factor). For this, we need experimental data such as the gold standard randomised double-blind placebo controlled trials. Is there such evidence in support of omega 3... oh, yes there is! A Scottish study conducted by Peet and Horrobin in 2002 took 70 patients who were suffering with persistent depression, despite receiving ongoing treatment. Participants were given either EPA or a placebo for 12 weeks. The group given EPA at a dosage range of 1g per day had significant improvements in the Hamilton Depression Rating Scale compared with those in the placebo group [3]. A 2009 review of three individual studies – one on EPA in bipolar depression, one on major childhood depression and one on unipolar adult depression – also demonstrated some promising results. In the adult study, significant positive benefits were found by week three compared to placebo. The bipolar depression patients showed a 50 per cent or greater reduction in Hamilton Depression Scale scores and the childhood depression participants displayed significant improvements in three rating scales in the treatment group [4]. These references could easily go on and on and I really encourage you to do some research and some digging to see just how broad and vast the evidence base is getting.

TRYPTOPHAN

Tryptophan has had quite a bit of press attention in recent years and its role in our mental health is significant. Tryptophan is an essential amino acid; we cannot make it ourselves, we have to get it from our diet. Like all amino acids, it is a building block in the manufacture of proteins, but it has another trick up its sleeve. Tryptophan is the chemical precursor to the feel-good neurotransmitter serotonin and consuming it can affect our mood.

Tryptophan crosses our blood brain barrier where it gets into the central nervous system (CNS). It goes through a sequence of transformation by enzymes, where it is converted into serotonin. However, there needs to be a catalyst to catapult tryptophan home into the CNS. That catalyst is a gentle insulin spike.

Long story short, to maximise this we need to eat a rich source of tryptophan with good-quality complex carbohydrate. An example could be an oat bar made with banana, a tuna open sandwich, or a turkey wrap. Something as simple as that. There are a lot of studies around that show positive results using tryptophan supplements, but these are not available in the UK. We have something called 5HTP (5-hydroxy tryptophan), a partially metabolised version of tryptophan, which can be highly effective. However, please note, from clinical experience I can tell you that this stuff is powerful! Please don't just take it willy-nilly. Work with a qualified practitioner who can ensure that you use this safely as well as effectively.

B VITAMINS

The B vitamins are one of the most important groups of nutrients and have numerous roles to play in the body, including important functions within the central nervous system.

B12 AND FOLIC ACID

B12 is probably most widely regarded for its role in the manufacture of red blood cells. It does, however, have a critical role to play in mental health, too. Firstly, B12 supports the functioning of myelin which, as we have seen (see page 15), is vital for communication between neurons. Even the slightest degradation or dysfunction of this can have a huge impact upon mood. B12 is also vital in the process of methylation, which marks genes for expression. This assists in the production and metabolism of neurotransmitters, hormone production and so on. B12 is also involved in the production of a type of neurotransmitter called monoamines. These are involved in emotion, cognition and arousal. Folic acid is another of the B vitamins that is associated with depression. There seems to be a link between folic acid and depression and there is a chain of thought that low levels of folic acid lead to low levels of a substance called SAMe (s adenosylmethionine), that is involved in neurotransmitter production and recycling. A 2005 review study found that both low folic acid and B12 were found in depressed patients and that adequate levels of these two nutrients were associated with better responsiveness to drug treatments and better treatment outcomes ⑤.

B6

When it comes to depression, I would say that vitamin B6 is up there on the 'essentials' list. As a nutrient it has two vital roles to play in the brain and both are extremely pertinent to depression. Firstly, B6 is involved in the formation of myelin. Secondly, and probably most importantly, is that B6 is vital for the conversion of tryptophan into serotonin. I have highlighted the importance of consuming foods rich in serotonin (see page 19). Well, that is half the battle. Once it gets through the blood brain barrier into the brain, it then needs to go through various steps of chemical conversion to become serotonin. B6 is involved in facilitating this.

ZINC

This is a nutrient that does not often get discussed in the press in terms of depression and mental health. This is a shame, as it seems to be one of the most critical in the whole picture. It is highly concentrated in our brains, with especially high concentrations in a region of the hippocampus. One of its jobs is to maintain the protective barrier that allows the right things to enter the brain, while stopping the wrong things. Zinc also modulates aspects of the stress response and seems to play a crucial role in neurological communication. Zinc is also an essential co-factor for hundreds of enzymatic reactions. Like omega 3, zinc has encouraging evidence to support its use in depression. Zinc deficiency has been found in several studies to induce depression, reduced focus and attention [6]. A 2013 randomised, double-blind, placebo-controlled trial that involved half of participants receiving 25mg of zinc alongside antidepressant SSRI drugs, and half receiving a placebo alongside drugs, showed that those in the treatment group had significantly reduced scores in the Beck Depression Inventory compared to the placebo group [7]. So this vital mineral should not be neglected.

BLOOD SUGAR BALANCE

I have touched on this before (see page 36) so I won't go overboard with it again, but blood sugar management is vital in managing depression. Keeping blood sugar levels stable influences our mood. There is no mistake there whatsoever. While not immediately associated with depression, keeping blood sugar even will make moods more stable, which will influence your outlook and the way you feel in general. The more stable and balanced you feel in terms of energy and mood, the better you will feel. Depression can affect the way in which you see the world around you. The more even you feel, the fewer extremes you will experience. OK, so there is less of a profound direct effect compared to the other nutritional elements I mentioned, but it is of value none the less.

NUTRITIONAL NUGGETS
TO AID DEPRESSION:

Eat plenty of oily fish such as salmon, mackerel and herrings
to get healthy helpings of pre-formed omega-3 fatty acids.
I recommend at least three or four servings a week, more
if you can manage it.

Eat turkey, tuna, bananas, eggs, spinach and game meats to
get plenty of the amino acid tryptophan. Make sure you eat
them with a complex carbohydrate, so mashed banana on
toast, open tuna sandwich and so on.

Eat plenty of green leafy vegetables, whole grains such as
brown rice, eggs, lean meats and fish to get a broad spectrum
of B vitamins, especially B12, B6 and folic acid.

Eat prawns, shellfish and pumpkin seeds for a good-quality
source of zinc.

Consider supplementing with omega 3. Look for a supplement
that contains at least 750mg of EPA and 250mg of DHA and
take this twice daily.

SAD

Seasonally affective disorder (SAD) is something that a few years ago was completely ridiculed, but in recent years has finally become accepted in mainstream medicine as something that is a genuine issue and is no fun for sufferers. Much of the advice that is appropriate for depression rings true for seasonal affective disorder and I would make exactly the same recommendations to anyone with SAD as I would with depression. But there is one little nugget that becomes specific here. That is....

VITAMIN D

Vitamin D has been a bit of a nutritional darling in recent years. What was once considered just a humble vitamin that was important for the health of our teeth and bones has now turned out to be something rather different. Rather than being a vitamin, vitamin D is actually more like a hormone and the broad spectrum of activities that have been attributed to it support this.

There is a growing link between vitamin D and depression. There are actually vitamin D receptors found in the brain. This tells us that vitamin D is obviously of extreme importance to some aspect of brain health. If it wasn't, those receptors would not be there. It is particularly interesting to note that these receptors are found in areas of the brain where depression arises.

So what exactly does vitamin D do in the brain and how might it help in depression? One theory is that it affects monoamine levels, which are important for stable mood, emotions and cognition. So what has seasonality got to do with all of this? Well, in lovely places such as California where it is beautiful and sunny and pretty consistent temperature-wise for most of the year, SAD just doesn't exist. Sure, depression still rears its ugly head. But not that fluctuating seasonal variety. Here in Britain on the other hand, well, it is rife! Why? Well the primary source of vitamin D for human beings is ultraviolet radiation hitting the skin and converting cholesterol into vitamin D precursors. So, as any Brit will attest, on that basis alone we are up the creek with not a paddle in sight. The lack of ultraviolet radiation exposure stops us naturally synthesising our own stores of vitamin D.

There are food sources of vitamin D, but these tend to be foods that are not eaten as much here. Full-fat milk, for example. Following the ridiculous low-fat farce that has dominated the public health messages of the last 30 years, people have moved over to semi-skimmed and skimmed milk. Guess where the vitamin D is? It is a fat-soluble nutrient so it is there in the fat, which gets taken away. Other sources of vitamin D include oily fish and offal.

So, as you can appreciate, here in the UK and nearby regions of Europe, we have something of a problem, because for most of the year the sun is merely a rumour. Without the right amount of sun exposure or an adequate intake of food sources of vitamin D, our levels will quickly plummet. It may seem unbelievable but, here in the UK, we are seeing rickets again. How that can happen in the modern age defies belief, but is testament to the deteriorating levels of vitamin D in our population.

A FINAL WORD

BRINGING EVERYTHING TOGETHER: THE NUTRITIONAL COMMONALITIES THAT CONNECT DIFFERENT CONDITIONS AND THE SIMILARITY IN TREATMENT

As you will have seen, the main conditions outlined in this book have their differences, but what is more starkly obvious is their similarities in terms of nutrition, what nutrients may benefit, how, and why. With that in mind, every recipe in this book will be of benefit right across the board. This may at first glance seem like a little bit of a blanket approach. But the similarity and overlap of nutritional approaches is really quite striking here. The elements that nutrition can control will be relevant for all issues discussed in this book. There are of course big differences in terms of changes in neurophysiology in each condition, but the similarities that they share in terms of the impact that diet can have upon them is really something. With this in mind, I personally feel that we need to take a step back. Let's look at the main areas of the nervous system that we know nutrition can influence and explore how we change our diets and manipulate nutrient intake. That is what I have done with this book. Nutrition will have its shortcomings in all these conditions and in no way would I suggest for a second that a change in diet is going to be some kind of magic bullet that will eradicate such issues. I do, however, strongly feel that the right dietary changes can have key influences upon neurophysiology in such a way as to offer notable benefits to these conditions. So, that is what I have done with the recipes in this book. These recipes bring together the best of this information. Rich in omega 3 fatty acids, B vitamins, key minerals and so on. This collection of dishes will provide the spectrum of nutrients that are beneficial to you, whichever of the issues discussed are a problem for you!

KEY INGREDIENTS FOR A HEALTHY NERVOUS SYSTEM

As we have seen on the previous pages, there are key differences between the mental health conditions described in terms of their nutritional management. However, there are some foods that are real champions when it comes to supporting the overall health of the nervous system as a whole and these should feature regularly on your shopping list.

BERRIES (DARK FRUITS)

Blueberries and blackberries. I am grouping these together as they both have almost identical properties. They are both very rich sources of a group of compounds called flavonoids. These have been shown to have significant effect upon the cardiovascular system and, as such, may have a positive impact upon the brain. What they do is cause blood vessels to relax, by stimulating the production of a chemical called nitric oxide by the vital inner skin that lines all of our blood vessels. Nitric oxide then causes the muscular walls of the blood vessels to relax, which makes the vessel wider. The consequence of this is that there is an important enhancement of circulation to the peripheries. Long story short, there is also, naturally, improved blood flow to the brain. Here in the UK, the University of Reading have been stuying this with some rather promising preliminary results.

COCOA

Who said that healthy food was never tasty? Well, hopefully reading through this book you will see that is certainly not the case. To take that one step further, I will be the bearer of great news: chocolate is good for you! There you go, what a revelation. OK... maybe I should back peddle a little and say that cocoa is good for you, especially for the health of our nervous systems and for making us feel really quite good. Firstly, cocoa contains very high levels of magnesium that helps us feel relaxed (see page 34). The most exciting thing, though, is a presence of something called PEA, or phenylethylamine. This is a neurotransmitter that is released in the brain when we fall in love and just a small amount can give us wonderful, welcome feelings of bliss and euphoria.

EGGS

Eggs are just a wonderful food. They are an incredible, complete protein. They are very low GI so can keep blood sugar levels nice and stable. They are also a very rich source of choline, which is important for memory and learning. You can also get eggs that have added omega 3; these will always be my top choice at the supermarket shelf.

KALE

Kale has become a bit of a buzz ingredient in the nutritional world of late. It is definitely the mothership of all green leafy vegetables. Kale, like all greens, is very dense in the mineral magnesium that can have a relaxing effect on the nervous system and the muscles (see page 34) so can really aid relaxation during a period of high anxiety. Kale also has good amounts of iron and vitamin C, to boot.

LENTILS

Lentils, like most legumes, are incredibly rich sources of most of the B vitamins, so provide a multitude of benefits for the brain and nervous systems, regulating many important functions.

MACKEREL

I just adore mackerel. It does have a strong flavour, so is one for the true fish fans. However, it is incredibly rich in omega 3 fatty acids and selenium and should be eaten at least once a week.

QUINOA

Quinoa is a funky little grain that makes a great alternative to rice. Refined carbohydrates such as white bread, white rice, white pasta, potatoes and so on all release their sugars very quickly, which causes an initial blood sugar rush; that quickly comes crashing down again once the body's insulin has dealt with it. This roller coaster of sugar highs and lows can play havoc with our moods and our ability to think clearly. Quinoa gives you a tasty, simple to prepare alternative that has a very low impact upon blood sugar and actually contains quite a lot of protein, too. This protein further slows down the release of sugars from its own carbs and those of whatever else you eat with it!

SALMON

One of my absolute favourite ingredients... in case you hadn't guessed. Salmon has to be one of the most palatable of the oily fish for most people. Versatile and packed with the all-important omega 3 fatty acids that support the health and functioning of the myelin sheath. Go for a mid-range pack of salmon; I personally tend to buy Scottish farmed fish.

SPINACH

Spinach is another real staple ingredient of mine. It is a great source of non-haem iron, and also of magnesium (see page 34); two vital minerals for the healthy functioning of the nervous system.

SWEET POTATO

Sweet potatoes are amazing. The taste is just so comforting. They make a great alternative to the regular spud, which is such a massive starch bomb and can send blood sugar levels soaring. Sweet potatoes have a much lower glycaemic response, so are the perfect option for baking, mashing, and even for chips. Honestly!

REFERENCES

Anxiety

① Kiecolt-Glaser JK, Belury MA, Andridge R, Malarkey WB, Glaser R. Omega 3 supplementation lowers inflammation and anxiety in medical students: a randomized controlled trial. Brain Behav Immun. 2011, 25(8): 1725-1734.

Depression

① Tanskanen A, Hibbeln JR, Tuomilehto J, Uutela A, Haukkala A, Viinamaki H, Lehtonen J, Vartiainen E. Fish consumption and depressive symptoms in the general population in Finland. Psychiatr Serv. 2001;52:529-531

② Silvers KM, Scott KM. Fish consumption and self-reported physical and mental health status. Public Health Nutr. 2002;5:427-431

③ Peet M, Horrobin DF. A dose ranging study of the effects of ethyl eicosapentaenoate in patients with ongoing depression despite adequate treatment with standard drugs. Arch Gen Psychiatry. 2002, 59(10): 913-919.

④ Osher Y, Belmaker RH. Omega 3 fatty acids in depression: a review of three studies. CNS Neurosci Ther. 2009, 15(2): 128-133.

⑤ Coppen A, Bolander-Gouaille C. Treatment of depression: time to consider folic acid and vitamin B12.

⑥ Nowak G, Szewczyk B, Pilc A. Zinc and depression: an update. Pharmacological reports. 2005, 57 713-718.

⑦ Ranjbar E, Kasaei MS, Mohammed-Shirazi M, Nasrollahzadeh J, Rashidkhani B, Shams J, Mostafavi SA, Mohammadi MR. Effects of zinc supplementation in patients with major depression: a randomised clinical trial. Iran J Psychiatry. 2013, 8(2): 73-79.

USEFUL CONTACTS AND RESOURCES

Anxiety UK
The main charity and support network for raising awareness and acceptance of anxiety. Packed with contacts, self-help techniques and useful information about multiple ways of managing anxiety, as well as chat forums and group support.

Mind UK
One of the best charitable resources for depression. Up-to-date information about campaigns, treatments, local events and group support.

Viridian Nutrition
An extensive range of the cleanest supplements around. Over 180 products including vitamins, minerals, herbs, oils and specific formulae made from the purest ingredients, with no additives, nasty fillers or junk. viridian-nutrition.com

RECIPES

Nutty Bircher muesli This is my take on a Bircher muesli. Packed with selenium and with a low GI, this is an ideal breakfast.

SERVES 1
4 heaped tbsp
    porridge oats
1 tbsp mixed seeds
    (pumpkin, flax,
    sunflower)
1 tbsp walnut pieces
1 tbsp broken brazil nuts
1 apple, chopped
3 tbsp natural yogurt

Mix all the ingredients together well in a breakfast bowl.

Eat! Feel free to change the types of nuts and seeds to suit your palate, or substitute the apple with a pear, if you like.

Greek omelette This is like a flavour explosion and is packed with all of my favourite things.

SERVES 1
4 handfuls of
   baby spinach
2–3 tsp olive oil
2 large eggs
a few small sprigs of dill
1 tbsp pitted kalamata
   olives, chopped
60g feta cheese

Sauté the spinach in a little of the oil, until it wilts. Set aside.

Pour the remaining oil into an omelette pan. Lightly beat the eggs and pour them into the pan. Once the eggs are almost completely cooked, spread the spinach across the middle. Add the dill and olives, crumble over the feta, and fold the omelette.

Cook for another two or three minutes to soften the cheese before turning out on to a plate.

Mackerel and garden pea frittata This sounds a little odd, I admit, but the sweetness of the peas really seems to match the strong flavour of the mackerel.

SERVES 1

2 tbsp garden peas
2–3 tsp olive oil
2 large eggs
1 cooked mackerel
    fillet, flaked

Preheat the grill. In a small ovenproof omelette pan, sauté the peas in the olive oil for one or two minutes. Whisk the eggs and add to the peas. Cook for three or four minutes, or until the egg is cooking around the edges, but the middle is still liquid.

Add the flaked mackerel, then place the pan under the hot grill until all the egg is cooked.

Smoked salmon, avocado mash and poached eggs on rye bread This is another great way of getting in omega 3 fatty acids and those all-important B vitamins.

SERVES 1

½ very ripe avocado
1 garlic clove,
    finely chopped
juice of ¼ lime
sea salt and freshly
    ground black pepper
splash of white
    wine vinegar
2 eggs
1 slice of pumpernickel
    bread
2 slices of smoked salmon
drizzle of olive oil

Begin by mashing the avocado flesh in a bowl. Add the garlic and lime juice with salt and pepper to taste.

Bring a pan of water to the boil. Add a splash of vinegar to the water, crack in the eggs and poach for around four minutes. Toast the pumpernickel bread.

Place the smoked salmon on the toasted bread and top with the avocado mash and then with the poached eggs. Drizzle with a little olive oil and add a little salt and pepper.

Eggs two ways My favourite breakfast is eggs royale, with eggs florentine in a very close second place. So I often make eggs two ways, to satisfy both cravings. I make no apology that I have published versions of these before; we all have our favourites and it just so happens that this wonderful combination contains many of the important nutrients for the health of the nervous system.

SERVES 1

2 handfuls of
   baby spinach
2 tsp olive oil
splash of white
   wine vinegar
3 large eggs
juice of ¼ lemon
75g butter
1 wholemeal
   English muffin
2 slices of
   smoked salmon

Quickly sauté the spinach in the olive oil, just long enough to wilt it. Set aside.

Bring a pan of water to the boil. Add a splash of vinegar to the water, crack in two of the eggs and poach for around four minutes.

Make the hollandaise: separate the remaining egg and put the yolk and lemon juice in a blender or food processor. Melt the butter in a pan. Switch the blender or processor on to a low setting to begin breaking up the egg and lemon juice. Add 1 tsp of the butter, then another. As the mixture begins to mix, slowly pour in the remaining butter. Once it has all been added, increase the speed to thicken the sauce.

Slice the muffin in two and toast both halves.

Place the smoked salmon on one muffin half, the spinach on the other, top both with the poached eggs, then smother in gorgeous hollandaise.

Breakfast smoothie bowl This is a great option when you want something that is relatively light, but slightly more exciting than just a drink. Smoothie bowls are basically thick smoothies that you can top with whatever. Use darker berries to get a potent flavonoid hit.

SERVES 1
2 handfuls of frozen
   mixed berries
100ml apple juice
1 tsp flax seeds
1 tsp pumpkin seeds
1 tsp broken walnuts
½ tsp desiccated coconut

Place the berries and juice into a reasonably powerful blender and blend into a thick smoothie. The texture will be thicker than the normal drinkable ones.

Transfer the smoothie to a serving bowl and sprinkle the remaining ingredients over.

Spiced lentil soup This is gorgeous and warming and the bowl is packed full of B vitamins and magnesium.

SERVES 1-2

1 large red onion,
   finely chopped
2 garlic cloves,
   finely chopped
1 tbsp olive oil
sea salt and freshly
   ground black pepper
½ tsp ground cumin
½ tsp turmeric
1 tsp ground cinnamon
150g red lentils
100g Puy lentils
800ml vegetable stock
   (you may not need
   all of this)

Sauté the onion and garlic in the olive oil with a good pinch of sea salt, until the onion has softened. Stir in the spices.

Add the lentils and enough stock to cover. Simmer until the Puy lentils are cooked. These will take longer to cook than the red lentils, which will virtually fall apart. I advise that you keep topping up the stock in order to maintain your desired thickness, as the mix will inevitably thicken as the red lentils cook down. Taste for seasoning and serve.

Salmon and avocado wasabi wrap

The flavours here are synonymous with sushi and it's a combination I love. This simple little lunch wrap will provide you with a massive omega 3 hit, magnesium, B vitamins and selenium.

SERVES 1
½ large ripe avocado
1–2 tsp wasabi, to taste
sea salt
1 large wholemeal
   tortilla wrap
4–5 slices of
   smoked salmon
handful of baby spinach
lime wedges, to serve
   (optional)

Scoop the avocado flesh into a bowl. Add the wasabi and a little sea salt and mash.

If you want a warm tortilla, heat a griddle pan over a high heat. Add the tortilla and heat through, turning once with tongs, until warm and marked with griddle marks.

Spread the wasabi avocado mixture across the tortilla. Place the salmon slices through the centre of the wrap. Top with the spinach and roll. Serve with lime wedges, if you like.

Steak salad This is just such a treat. I don't eat masses of red meat, but a steak every now and again can give you such an iron fix that it will really last. The vitamin C in the spinach leaves and dressing increase your absorption of it, too! A winner all round.

SERVES 1

For the dressing
2 tsp horseradish sauce
juice of ½ lemon
1 tbsp extra virgin
   olive oil

For the salad
1 sirloin steak
2 handfuls of
   baby spinach
handful of pea shoots
3–4 radishes, sliced

Combine the dressing ingredients and whisk well to form an emulsion.

Cook the steak according to your preference, then leave it to rest for five minutes. Slice.

Combine the leaves, shoots and radishes, top with the steak and drizzle with the dressing.

Cobb salad This is one of my favourite salads. A traditional cobb includes bacon, but I have left it out here. If you can find a decent organic bacon without nitrates, then feel free to add it. I have also gone for a balsamic dressing to keep it a little lighter, rather than cobb salad's usual ranch-style. This salad will seriously fill you up!

SERVES 1

For the salad
2 large handfuls of
   mixed salad leaves
1 large cooked
   chicken breast
2 hard-boiled eggs
½ very ripe avocado
50g Danish blue cheese

For the dressing
1 tsp balsamic vinegar
1 tbsp extra virgin
   olive oil
sea salt and freshly
   ground black pepper

Place the leaves on a plate. Slice the chicken and the eggs. Chop the avocado into small cubes. Place these all on top of the leaves and crumble on the blue cheese.

Combine the dressing ingredients and whisk well to an emulsion. Dress with the dressing.

Warm roasted vegetable and feta salad

This is glorious at any time of year. The bright, vibrant colours make it a great summer dish but, as it is served warm and bursting with flavour, it is equally satisfying in the cooler months.

SERVES 1

1 courgette, sliced
   into rounds
1 large red pepper,
   chopped into
   bite-sized pieces
1 large red onion,
   halved then sliced
4–5 mushrooms, sliced
olive oil
½ tsp garlic granules
½ tsp smoked paprika
sea salt and freshly
   ground black pepper
leaves from a small
   bunch of curly parsley,
   coarsely chopped
80g feta cheese

Preheat the oven to 200°C/400°F/gas mark 6.

Place the vegetables in a roasting tin, drizzle with a little olive oil and toss well. Sprinkle over the garlic granules and paprika, season to taste with salt and pepper and toss well again.

Place at the top of the hot oven, and roast for 20–25 minutes, stirring frequently.

Place the roasted vegetables on to a serving plate, sprinkle over the parsley, then crumble over the feta.

Satay prawns and greens Trust me, this dish has such an addictive quality... you'll be doing back flips that it is actually good for you, too! We used intact prawns for the photo, but buy those without heads or shells, if you prefer.

SERVES 1

1 large red onion,
    halved then sliced
2 garlic cloves,
    finely chopped
1 red chilli,
    finely chopped
1 tbsp olive oil
sea salt
2 handfuls of greens
    (I prefer spring greens
    or similar), shredded
80g cooked king prawns,
    deveined if necessary
1 heaped tbsp
    peanut butter
1 tsp honey
3 tsp soy sauce
½ tsp Chinese
    5-spice powder

Sauté the onion, garlic and chilli in the oil with a good pinch of sea salt, until the onion softens.

Add the greens and continue to stir-fry until they turn a brighter green and begin to soften.

Add the prawns, peanut butter, honey, soy sauce and 5-spice and mix well before serving.

Spinach and mixed bean quesadillas

These are a great option for those days when you could eat a horse and chase the jockey. They are seriously filling and packed with B vitamins to boot! Quesadillas are usually made in a frying pan, but I prefer them cooked in the oven; they just get a little crisper.

SERVES 1

2 handfuls of
    baby spinach
2 tsp olive oil
400g can of mixed beans,
    drained and rinsed
¼ tsp ground cumin
sea salt
2 small wholemeal
    tortilla wraps
handful of grated
    Cheddar cheese

Preheat the oven to 200°C/400°F/gas mark 6.

Quickly sauté the spinach in the olive oil, just long enough to wilt it. Add the beans, mix well, then partially mash/smash the mixture with the back of a fork. Add the cumin and a little sea salt.

Spread the bean mixture on to one of the tortillas. Sprinkle over the Cheddar and place the other tortilla on top. Place on a baking sheet and bake at the top of the hot oven for about eight minutes: long enough for the cheese to melt and the tortillas to begin to get crispy.

Cut into triangles and serve.

Sourdough California crostini These are just epic! I am very possibly addicted to sushi and one of my favourites is the California roll, with its combination of salmon and avocado. This is a great way to recreate the sushi flavour experience without having to get all creative with the bamboo mats. When buying fish to make your own sashimi, please ensure that it is fresh and from the fish counter. Ask the fishmonger to skin it, too, and triple-check the freshness if need be.

SERVES 1
1 small very ripe avocado
1 tsp wasabi paste
2–3 tsp soy sauce
1 salmon fillet, skinned
    by the fishmonger
1 slice of sourdough bread

Scoop the flesh from the avocado into a bowl. Add the wasabi and soy sauce and mash, ensuring an even mixture.

Slice the salmon fillet into thin (½–1cm) slices.

Toast the sourdough bread. Top with the avocado mixture. Lay the salmon slices on top and serve.

Broccoli and Stilton soup This soup is a real classic and needs little introduction from me. Magnesium, B vitamins and calcium are the key nutrients here.

SERVES 2
1 onion, finely chopped
1 celery stick, finely sliced
1 leek, finely sliced
2 tbsp olive oil
sea salt
1 potato, peeled
    and chopped
1 head of broccoli,
    broken into
    small florets
1 litre vegetable stock
150g Stilton cheese

Sauté the onion, celery and leek in the oil, with a good pinch of sea salt, until all the vegetables have become soft.

Add the potato and broccoli and cover with the stock. Simmer for 10–15 minutes, until the broccoli and potato have softened.

Crumble in most of the Stilton, leaving just a small piece behind. Transfer to a blender, or use a hand-held blender, to blend into a thick soup.

Mix in the remaining Stilton before serving.

King prawn and guacamole open sandwich

This gorgeous lunch packs a serious nutritional punch. Selenium, magnesium, B vitamins... It definitely ticks the right boxes.

SERVES 1

½ very ripe avocado
1 garlic clove,
    finely chopped
½ red chilli,
    finely chopped
juice of ½ lime
sea salt and freshly
    ground black pepper
1 slice of rye bread
75g cooked king prawns,
    deveined if necessary
drizzle of olive oil

Scoop the flesh of the avocado into a bowl and add the garlic, chilli, lime juice, plus salt and pepper to taste. Mash into a coarse guacamole.

Toast the rye bread.

Spread the avocado mixture over the toasted rye bread. Top with the king prawns. Add a little black pepper, then drizzle with olive oil.

Gorgeous green soup I know, eating greens isn't always the most exciting thing in the world. But this soup really does bring them to life. Even kids love this one... if that's not testament to the flavour, I don't know what is!

SERVES 1–2

1 onion, finely chopped
1 garlic clove,
   finely chopped
1 tbsp olive oil
sea salt
350g fresh or frozen peas
1 large courgette,
   roughly chopped
1 large potato,
   skin-on, chopped
500ml vegetable stock
200g bag of baby spinach

Sauté the onion and garlic in the olive oil with a pinch of sea salt, until the onion softens.

Add the peas, courgette and potato, then pour in enough vegetable stock to just cover all the ingredients. Simmer until the potato softens.

Add the baby spinach a handful at a time, until it has all wilted into the mix.

Blend the soup until smooth, then serve.

Rainbow houmous pitta pockets

Rainbow houmous pitta pockets I got the idea for these from an old sandwich bicycle delivery company that used to deliver to a clinic where I worked. Simple, but so moreish it is unreal, plus they tick almost every box for supporting nervous system health: B vitamins, magnesium, flavonoids... and low GL to boot!

SERVES 1

1 small carrot, grated
1 small raw beetroot, grated
1 spring onion, chopped
3 tbsp houmous
1 small wholemeal pitta bread

Mix the carrot, beetroot and spring onion together, then add the houmous and mix well.

Gently warm the pitta bread, then slice straight through the middle to give you two pockets.

Tease open the pockets and stuff with the houmous mixture.

Perfect wrapped up for lunch on the go, or served with a salad.

Grilled halloumi with pomegranate quinoa salad

This is a nice filling lunch, perfect for those days when you may not get a chance to eat until quite late and you want to fill up but keep it healthy, too. It will stabilise your blood sugar and provide a B vitamin boost. Ready-prepared pomegranate is readily available in supermarkets now, so is hassle-free.

SERVES 1

50g quinoa
2 tbsp pomegranate
   seeds
1 tbsp pitted black
   olives, chopped
leaves from a small bunch
   of parsley, chopped
sea salt and freshly
   ground black pepper
4 slices of halloumi
   cheese
a little olive oil

Place the quinoa in a saucepan and cover with boiling water. Simmer for around 20 minutes, until the quinoa is softened and a small tail has formed on the grain (I'm not making it up!). Drain.

Mix the quinoa with the pomegranate seeds, olives and parsley, with a little salt and pepper.

Place the halloumi on a lightly oiled griddle pan or frying pan and lightly fry for two or three minutes each side, until turning golden brown.

Serve the halloumi on top of the quinoa with a mixed leaf salad.

Roasted sweet potato salad with green dressing

This dish was one of those wonderful happy discoveries that arise when there are left over odds and ends in the fridge that need using. The dressing sounds weird but, my word, it is flavour central!

SERVES 1

For the salad
1 small sweet potato,
    skin-on, chopped
1–2 tsp olive oil
sea salt and freshly
    ground black pepper
2 handfuls of mixed
    salad leaves
60g feta cheese
1 tsp pine nuts

For the green dressing
½ very ripe avocado
1 tsp white vinegar
    or cider vinegar
1 small garlic clove,
    chopped
15g bunch of coriander

Preheat the oven to 200°C/400°F/gas mark 6.

Place the sweet potato on a baking tray, drizzle with the oil, sprinkle over a little sea salt and bake for 20–30 minutes. I like the pieces to begin to caramelise on the edges.

To make the dressing, place the avocado flesh, vinegar, garlic, coriander and 2–3 tbsp of water in a blender, add salt and pepper to taste and blend into a smooth, luminous dressing.

Combine the roasted sweet potato and salad leaves in a serving bowl. Crumble over the feta.

Pour over the dressing and toss, then sprinkle with the pine nuts to serve.

Sesame coated tuna steak with broad bean, lime and coriander stir-fry This has a lovely Asian/European fusion thing going on. I love combining multiple influences, it opens up a whole new world of cuisine.

SERVES 1
1 leek, sliced
2 garlic cloves,
    finely sliced
1 tbsp olive oil
sea salt
300g canned broad
    beans, drained
2 handfuls of
    baby spinach
1 tsp soy sauce
juice of ½ lime
1 sprig of coriander
4–5 tbsp sesame seeds
1 tuna steak

Sauté the leek and garlic in the oil, with a good pinch of sea salt, until the leek has softened.

Add the broad beans and spinach and stir-fry until the spinach has wilted. Add the soy sauce and lime juice, then tear in the coriander. Mix well, then set aside.

Sprinkle the sesame seeds out over a large plate. Roll the tuna steak through the seeds several times to ensure it is fully coated.

Gently fry the tuna steak over a low heat (so the seeds do not brown too much) for five minutes, turning. This will give the tuna a seared/pinky finish at this temperature. If you prefer your tuna cooked more thoroughly, keep going for longer, turning regularly.

Warm through the broad bean stir-fry, then place in the centre of the serving plate. Cut the tuna steak in half to reveal the pink centre, then lay the two halves over the stir-fry. Serve.

Mediterranean salmon with curly kale and sweet potato mash

This is such a delightful dish and an absolute nutrient bath, too! Carotenoids, magnesium, omega 3 fatty acids, flavonoids... this has it all.

SERVES 2

1 large red onion, finely chopped
2 garlic cloves, finely chopped
1 red pepper, finely chopped
1 tbsp olive oil
sea salt and freshly ground black pepper
400g can of chopped tomatoes
1 tbsp pitted black olives, chopped
2 salmon fillets
1 large sweet potato, peeled and finely chopped
4 handfuls of curly kale

Preheat the oven to 200°C/400°F/gas mark 6.

Sauté the onion, garlic and pepper in the oil, with a pinch of sea salt, until the onion and pepper begin to soften. Add the tomatoes and olives, bring to the boil, then reduce the heat and allow to simmer for 25–30 minutes. The sauce will reduce and begin to resemble a ratatouille. Taste and season again if necessary.

Place the salmon on a baking sheet and bake at the top of the oven for 15–20 minutes, until cooked throughout and turning golden at the edges. Be sure to check on it during cooking.

Meanwhile, place the sweet potato in a saucepan and cover with boiling water. Simmer for around 15 minutes, until soft enough to fall apart under a fork. Drain and mash, adding a little salt and pepper to taste. (You can also jazz this up by adding mustard, or soft goat's cheese.) Steam the kale over boiling water for a few minutes, until tender (it will turn a brighter green).

Serve the mash and kale on plates. Lay the salmon across and top with the pepper sauce.

Wholewheat pasta with walnut pesto and baby spinach

I'm not a fan of excessive carbohydrate consumption, but with issues such as anxiety and depression a good carb injection once or twice a week can be very helpful. This is because carbs, alongside the amino acid tryptophan (found here in the walnuts), can increase serotonin production, which can lift mood and regulate sleep. In itself not a miracle cure, this is nevertheless an important part of the overall picture.

SERVES 2

150g wholewheat
    fusilli or penne
175g walnuts
125g basil leaves
3 garlic cloves
2 tbsp grated hard
    goat's cheese
200ml olive oil
sea salt and freshly
    ground black pepper
4 large handfuls of
    baby spinach

Place the pasta in a saucepan and top with boiling water. Simmer for 12–15 minutes, until the pasta is ready. Drain.

Meanwhile, place all the remaining ingredients except the spinach into a food processor and process on a medium speed to a coarse pesto.

Wilt the spinach in a pan in 2 tbsp of boiling water in the same way as you would in olive oil: just 'sauté' until it wilts. Stir in the cooked pasta and mix well. Add pesto to taste (any left over is amazing on toast with avocado) and mix well.

Thai-style seafood noodle soup

I love these types of soups. My many escapades in Asia have allowed me to try all kinds of styles and flavours of noodle soups. From curry laksa to miso ramen, I love them all. This is super-flavoursome and packed with omega 3. Soba noodles come in pre-portioned bundles. Check the noodle packet, as lots of the more readily available soba noodles contain wheat.

SERVES 2

2 bundles of soba noodles
1 lemon grass stalk
½ red onion,
    finely chopped
1 garlic clove,
    finely chopped
1cm root ginger, peeled
    and finely chopped
2 kaffir lime leaves
1 tbsp olive oil
400g can of coconut milk
2 salmon fillets, skinned
    and cubed
handful of spinach
2 handfuls of cooked
    prawns, deveined
    if necessary
juice of ½ lime
handful of coriander
    leaves, torn

Place the soba noodles in a saucepan, top with boiling water and allow to simmer for about 12 minutes, until the noodles are soft. Set aside.

Bash the lemon grass stalk with something heavy, such as a rolling pin, to release all the fragrant oils. Add it to a pan with the onion, garlic, ginger and kaffir lime leaves and sauté in the olive oil until the onion is soft.

Add the coconut milk and 150ml of water and cook on a slow simmer for 15 minutes. Throw in the salmon and the spinach leaves and continue to simmer until the salmon is cooked (about 10 minutes). Add the prawns.

Drain the soba noodles. Divide them between two bowls, top with the soup, squeeze in the lime juice and add the coriander.

Tandoori salmon with saag dal

What a combination, both in terms of flavour and nutrient composition. This is almost the perfect dish for the nervous system: omega 3; B vitamins; magnesium; low GI. I use shop-bought tandoori paste here as it really does save you a lot of time!

SERVES 2

4 heaped tsp
    tandoori paste
8 tsp natural yogurt
2 salmon fillets
2 garlic cloves,
    finely chopped
1 tbsp olive or coconut oil
sea salt and freshly
    ground black pepper
130g red lentils
1 litre vegetable stock
    (you may not use
    all of it)
260g baby spinach
½ tsp turmeric
¼ tsp ground cumin

Preheat the oven to 180°C/350°F/gas mark 4.

Mix the tandoori paste and yogurt together. Place the salmon fillets on a baking tray and top with the yogurt mixture. Place at the top of the oven and bake for 25–30 minutes.

Meanwhile, sauté the garlic in the olive or coconut oil, with a good pinch of salt, over a very high heat. This is one occasion where you want the garlic to brown; this gives it a distinctive smoky flavour that makes the dal amazing.

Add the lentils and a small amount of vegetable stock. Keep adding stock every few minutes, as the lentils cook down, adding it little and often until the mix has a porridge-like texture.

Add the baby spinach and cook until it wilts, then measure in the turmeric and cumin and mix. Taste and season as needed, then serve.

Beetroot, goat's cheese and walnut flatbread with rocket

This is a nice decadent weekend dish. It is very nutritious, but a bit on the naughty side, too. I'm a firm believer in having your cake and eating it now and again.

SERVES 2

250g wholemeal flour
2 tbsp flax seeds
250g cooked beetroot, chopped
150g soft goat's cheese
7–8 tsp crème fraîche
2 tbsp walnut pieces
2 large handfuls of rocket leaves
a little balsamic glaze, to serve

Preheat the oven to 180°C/350°F/gas mark 4.

Combine the flour and seeds with 120–130ml of warm water. Mix into a dough and knead well. Roll out into a rectangular flatbread no more than 5mm thick. Place on a baking tray and bake at the top of the oven for about 15 minutes, or until almost cooked and beginning to turn golden in places. Remove from the oven.

Top with the beetroot and crumble over the goat's cheese, filling as many gaps between the beetroot as possible. Then add the crème fraîche in small dollops, again ensuring it is well spread out and filling as many gaps as possible. You need to think that every bite should contain beetroot, cheese and crème fraîche.

Sprinkle over the walnuts and return to the oven for another eight to 10 minutes, or until the cheese is turning golden and very soft.

Remove from the oven, scatter over the rocket leaves, then drizzle over a generous helping of balsamic glaze.

Steak with mashed peas, green beans and courgettes

This is a heavenly dish. Great in the summer months al fresco, or satisfying in the winter with a few cooked root vegetables alongside. There's masses of iron and magnesium in this.

SERVES 2

200g garden peas
1 large courgette,
    cut into rounds
100g green beans
1 tbsp olive oil
2 sirloin steaks
100g feta cheese
freshly ground
    black pepper

Place the peas in a saucepan, cover with boiling water and simmer until they soften.

Sauté the courgette and green beans in the olive oil until the courgette softens and the beans have turned a brighter green and softened slightly, but still retain their bite.

Cook the steaks according to your preferences.

Mash the peas, then combine them with the beans and courgette. Crumble in the feta, season with some black pepper and toss well. Serve with the sliced steak on top.

Pesto flax-crusted salmon with minted butter greens

This is oozing with good fats and magnesium. Rich, flavoursome and really easy to prepare. Don't be afraid of using butter, it's a million times better for you than vegetable oils and margarines!

SERVES 2

1½ tbsp pesto
2 tbsp ground flax seed
2 salmon fillets
4 large handfuls of chard or spring greens, shredded
35g butter
200g garden peas
leaves from a few mint sprigs, chopped
sea salt and freshly ground black pepper

Preheat the oven to 200°C/400°F/gas mark 6.

Mix the pesto and ground flax seed together to form a paste.

Place the salmon fillets on a baking tray and bake at the top of the oven for around eight minutes. Remove, top with the pesto mixture and return to the oven for a final 10 minutes.

Place the greens, butter and peas in a pan. Sauté over a medium heat for eight to 10 minutes, until the greens have wilted and the peas are beginning to soften.

Add the mint, season with salt and pepper and mix well. Serve with the salmon.

Mackerel with herbed mixed bean salad

Another super-filling yet light dinner, with lots of B vitamins, selenium, zinc and, of course, the ever-faithful omega 3.

SERVES 2

2 x 400g cans of mixed beans, drained and rinsed
6–7 cherry tomatoes, halved or quartered
¼ red onion, finely chopped
2 tsp capers, drained and rinsed
leaves from a small bunch of parsley, roughly chopped
juice of ½ lemon, plus lemon slices (optional)
sea salt and freshly ground black pepper
2 mackerel fillets
2–3 tsp olive oil

Tip the beans into a bowl. Add the tomatoes, onion, capers and parsley and squeeze over the lemon juice. Season with salt and pepper and mix well.

If you want, you can cover the skin side of the fish fillets with lemon slices now, though it makes them tougher to turn in the pan! Lightly fry the mackerel fillets in the oil for five or six minutes, turning frequently, to give you a nice seared fish. Serve with the bean salad.

Fabulous fish pie

This is fabulous feel-good food at its best. The fact that it is packed to the hilt with important nutrients for the nervous system is a massive bonus. But it tastes so good, that will be the last thing on your mind!

SERVES 2
2½ large sweet potatoes
½ onion, finely chopped
1 garlic clove,
    finely chopped
1 tbsp olive oil
sea salt and freshly
    ground black pepper
200g low-fat soft cheese
100ml vegetable stock
2 tsp wholegrain mustard
400g fish pie mix
10g dill, roughly chopped

Peel the sweet potatoes and chop them. Place in a saucepan, cover with boiling water and simmer for around 20 minutes, until very soft. Preheat the oven to 200°C/400°F/gas mark 6.

Sauté the onion and garlic in the olive oil, with a pinch of sea salt, until the onion softens. Add the soft cheese, stock and mustard to the pan and mix well over a medium heat. Add the fish pie mix and simmer for 10 minutes, until most of the fish is cooked. Add the dill and mix well.

Transfer the mixture to a baking dish. Mash the sweet potato into a smooth mash, seasoning with salt and pepper to taste.

Top the fish with the sweet potato mash and bake at the top of the oven for about 15 minutes, until the sauce is bubbling and the top of the mash is starting to get crispy.

Fried mackerel fillets on beetroot-horseradish crush

Heaven! These three magic ingredients combine to make a flavour trio that becomes quite addictive.

SERVES 2

2 mackerel fillets
sea salt and freshly
    ground black pepper
2 tsp olive oil
400g cooked beetroot,
    chopped
3 tsp horseradish sauce
juice of ½ lemon
leaves from a small
    bunch of dill or parsley,
    roughly chopped

Season the mackerel fillets with a little salt and pepper and lightly fry in the olive oil for around eight minutes, turning regularly.

Mix the beetroot, horseradish sauce, lemon juice and herbs. Divide into two portions.

Place a portion of the beetroot-horseradish crush on a plate and top with a mackerel fillet.

Serve with steamed greens or sweet potato wedges on the side.

Honey mustard-glazed salmon with squash purée, garlic kale and avocado salsa

This dish was inspired by a glorious creation I had in a well-known southern California seafood restaurant chain. Such a beautiful combination of flavours and almost every important nutrient for the health of the nervous system.

SERVES 2
2 salmon fillets
2 tsp honey
1 tsp mustard
2 tsp soy sauce
½ onion, finely chopped
4 tsp olive oil
sea salt
½ butternut squash, peeled and chopped
300ml vegetable stock (you may not need it all)
4 large handfuls of chard, shredded
2 garlic cloves, finely chopped
½ very ripe avocado
4–5 cherry tomatoes, chopped
1 tsp balsamic vinegar

Preheat the oven to 200°C/400°F/gas mark 6.

Place the salmon in a small roasting tin. Make the glaze by mixing the honey, mustard and soy sauce together with 2 tsp of water. Pour the glaze over the salmon and roast at the top of the hot oven for about 20 minutes. Keep checking it regularly and spoon back over any glaze that has run off the salmon. It will caramelise more and more as the cooking continues.

Sauté the onion in 2 tsp of the olive oil, with a pinch of sea salt, until it softens. Add the squash and enough stock to partially cover. Simmer for about 15 minutes, until softened. Transfer to a blender or food processor and purée.

Stir fry-the greens and garlic in the remaining 2 tsp of olive oil for around five minutes, until the greens wilt. Chop the avocado and add the tomatoes and balsamic vinegar to make a salsa.

Place a serving of purée and a serving of greens side by side. Top with the salmon, then place a couple of teaspoons of the salsa on top.

Sweet potato, kale and red lentil stew

This is big time comfort food. Seriously filling, yet it won't stick to your ribs. Masses of B vitamins, magnesium and other goodies.

SERVES 2

1 large red onion,
   finely chopped
2 garlic cloves,
   finely chopped
1 tbsp olive oil
sea salt
1 heaped tbsp miso paste
1 large sweet potato,
   skin-on, chopped
300g red lentils
4–5 large handfuls
   of curly kale

Begin by sautéing the onion and garlic in the olive oil, with a pinch of sea salt, until the onion has softened. Add the miso paste and stir well.

Now tip in the sweet potato and the lentils, with enough hot water to just cover the pan contents.

Simmer until the lentils have mostly broken down and the sweet potato has softened. You may need to add more water as you go. The end consistency should resemble porridge.

At this stage, add the kale and continue to simmer until the kale has softened and wilted.

Green crumble I know this sounds a bit hippyish, but it really is a very moreish dish; even the most hardcore vegetable dodgers seem to warm to this one. Magnesium and B vitamin-packed.

SERVES 2

570g mixed green vegetables (leeks, peas, courgettes and cabbage work well)
42g garlic butter
leaves from a small bunch of parsley, roughly chopped
leaves from a few sprigs of mint, chopped
sea salt and freshly ground black pepper
porridge oats (no need to weigh, you'll see why)
3–4 tsp finely grated Parmesan cheese

Preheat the oven to 190°C/375°F/gas mark 5.

Sauté the green vegetables in the garlic butter for eight to 10 minutes, until all the vegetables begin to soften. Stir in the herbs and season with a little salt and pepper.

Transfer the greens to a baking dish. Now it is time to add the oats. The reason I don't bother with weight here is that there is so much variation in baking dish size; being too rigid with weight can lead to an oat layer that is way too thick or too thin. So, sprinkle enough oats over the top to give you a topping about 5mm thick. Sprinkle over the Parmesan and season with a little salt and pepper.

Bake at the top of the oven for about 15 minutes, or until the crumble is golden and crunchy. Serve with a side salad.

Chicken satay skewers with cashew quinoa and red cabbage sesame salad

I'm a real lover of satay. It is traditionally served with cubes of compacted white rice, known as *ketupat*. I've opted for quinoa here instead, to make it a nice slow burner.

SERVES 2

*For the chicken
    and quinoa*
1 large skinless chicken
    breast, chopped
sea salt and freshly
    ground black pepper
50g (dry weight) quinoa
2 tsp vegetable
    bouillon powder
3 tbsp grated red cabbage
1 tsp mayonnaise
1 tsp soy sauce
1 tsp sesame seeds
6–8 cashew nuts

For the satay sauce
1 heaped tbsp
    peanut butter
1 tsp honey
2–3 tsp soy sauce
¼ tsp Chinese
    5-spice powder
1 garlic clove,
    finely chopped
½ chilli, finely chopped

Preheat the oven to 200°C/400°F/gas mark 6.

Thread the chicken on to two metal skewers. Season with salt and pepper, place on a foil-lined baking tray and bake for around 25 minutes, turning occasionally.

Place the quinoa and bouillon powder into a saucepan, top with just-boiled water and allow to simmer for around 25 minutes. The quinoa should soften and little 'tails' should form on the side of it. Drain and set aside.

Mix the cabbage, mayonnaise, soy sauce and all the sesame seeds together to make a coleslaw-type salad.

Mix all the satay sauce ingredients together in a small bowl with 3–4 tbsp of hot water. When you first add them together, the ingredients may look like they have separated. This is normal. Mix well and they combine beautifully.

Place the quinoa in the centre of the plate and break the cashews over it. Lay the chicken skewers on top of it, then smother with the sauce. Place the cabbage salad to the side.

Salmon with courgette ribbons, spinach and a red pepper-pine nut sauce

This is a complete flavour bomb. There is a fair bit to do here, so this recipe is perfect for days when you have a little more time on your hands. I love this on a Friday evening.

SERVES 1

For the sauce
1 red pepper, deseeded and sliced
2 tbsp olive oil
sea salt and freshly ground black pepper
1 tbsp pine nuts
2 tsp grated Parmesan cheese
1 garlic clove, chopped

For the rest
1 large courgette
½ onion, finely sliced
½ tbsp olive oil
2 handfuls of baby spinach
1 salmon fillet

Preheat the oven to 200°C/400°F/gas mark 6.

Start with the sauce first. Place the pepper on a baking tray and drizzle with half the olive oil. Season with a little salt and pepper and roast for 20–25 minutes, until soft and the edges are beginning to caramelise. Leave the oven on.

Transfer the peppers to a food processor. Add the pine nuts, Parmesan, garlic and remaining 1 tbsp of olive oil and blitz into a luscious sauce.

Cut the courgette into ribbons using a vegetable peeler. Sauté the onion and courgette in the ½ tbsp of olive oil until the onion has softened and the courgette is soft and a brighter green. Add the baby spinach and continue to sauté until it wilts. Set aside.

Place the salmon on a baking tray. Season with salt and pepper and bake for 12–15 minutes.

Warm through the courgette mix, then stir in the sauce. Plate the vegetables up in the centre of a serving plate and top with the salmon.

Salmon skewers with wasabi root vegetable mash Rich, flavoursome, easy comfort food at its best.

SERVES 2

2 tbsp soy sauce
1 tsp honey
½ tsp Chinese 5-spice powder
2 salmon fillets, skinned and cut into chunks
2 parsnips, peeled and chopped
1 large sweet potato, peeled and chopped
2 tsp wasabi, or to taste
sea salt
julienned spring onion, to serve (optional)

Mix the soy sauce, honey and 5-spice together. Add the salmon, stir well and allow to marinate for one hour. If using wooden or bamboo skewers, soak them for 30 minutes, so they won't scorch in the pan or under the grill.

Place the parsnips and sweet potato in a pan and cover with boiling water. Simmer for about 15 minutes, or until the vegetables are soft enough to mash.

Mash the vegetables. Add the wasabi and season with a little salt, stir well, then set aside.

Thread the salmon on to skewers, roll in the marinade once more, then either fry or cook under a preheated grill, turning frequently.

Warm through the mash and serve the skewers on top of the mash, sprinkled with julienned spring onion, if you like. This is great with steamed greens or a side salad.

Kway teow In my many travels, I have been lucky enough to spend a good chunk of time in Malaysia. One of my favourite dishes is a noodle dish called *char kway teow*, basically stir-fried rice noodles with all manner of bits and bobs thrown in. Seriously tasty, easy and a great way to use up odd bits in the fridge.

SERVES 1

50g (dry weight) flat rice noodles
1 large red onion, halved, then sliced
1 large spring onion, cut lengthways
2 garlic cloves, finely chopped
½ red chilli, finely chopped
1 tbsp olive oil
sea salt
100g cooked king prawns, shelled and deveined if necessary
3 tsp soy sauce
1 tsp toasted sesame oil
1 egg

Place the rice noodles in a bowl and pour boiling water over them. Leave to soften for five to eight minutes.

Stir-fry the onion, spring onion, garlic and chilli in the olive oil, along with a little sea salt, until the onion is soft.

Add the prawns. Drain the noodles, then add them to the pan and mix together thoroughly.

Add the soy sauce and sesame oil and mix well.

Finally, crack the egg in and stir through the noodles until it has a scrambled egg-like texture.

Chicken and spinach burgers These unusual looking burgers are great: nutrient-packed yet very light, full of magnesium and with loads of high-quality protein.

SERVES 2
½ red onion,
    finely chopped
1 large garlic clove,
    finely chopped
½ tbsp olive oil
sea salt and freshly
    ground black pepper
4 handfuls of spinach
2 skinless chicken
    breasts, chopped
1 egg

Sauté the onion and garlic in the olive oil, with a pinch of sea salt, until the onion softens. Add the spinach and continue to sauté until it has wilted. Allow to cool.

Put the chicken breast in a food processor with the spinach mixture. Season with salt and pepper. Crack in the egg, then process into a thick, green, mince-like texture. Preheat your grill to its highest setting.

Form the mixture into burger patties and place them on a foil-lined baking tray, then under the preheated grill. Grill for 15–20 minutes, turning regularly, to ensure they are cooked throughout.

These can be served in a burger bun, or with salad or cooked vegetables.

Pistachio-crusted mackerel with green rice

Green rice is just brown rice with very finely chopped herbs mixed through it. The end result is a very colourful side dish. This looks and sounds fancy, but is really easy!

SERVES 2
140g brown basmati rice
100g shelled pistachios
2 tbsp oatmeal
½ tsp dried mixed herbs
½ tsp garlic powder
sea salt and freshly
    ground black pepper
2 tsp olive oil
2 mackerel fillets
small bunch of coriander
small bunch of basil

Place the brown rice in a pan, cover with boiling water and simmer for 20–25 minutes, until the rice has softened. Preheat the oven to 200°C/400°F/gas mark 6.

Place the pistachios, oatmeal, dried mixed herbs, garlic powder and a little salt and pepper into a food processor and process to a coarse mixture. Add the olive oil and process again.

Place the mackerel fillets on a baking tray and bake at the top of the hot oven for 10 minutes. Remove, then top with the pistachio mixture. Return to the oven for another 10 minutes, until the pistachio crust is just turning golden.

Finely chop the coriander and basil, as small as you can get it. Strain the rice, mix the chopped herbs into it and season. Serve the mackerel with the rice and a side salad.

Baked ratatouille

This is one of my favourite dinners for those days when you want some oozing comfort food, but don't want to faff around in the kitchen for hours on end. The fact that it is packed with flavonoids, magnesium and is low GL is just the icing on the cake!

SERVES 1

1 large red onion, finely chopped
2 garlic cloves, finely chopped
1 tbsp olive oil
sea salt
1 large red pepper, deseeded and chopped
1 large courgette, sliced
400g can of chopped tomatoes
3 handfuls of grated cheese

Sauté the onion and garlic in the olive oil, with a little sea salt, for three to five minutes. Add the pepper and courgette and continue to sauté for about five minutes. Preheat the oven to 200°C/400°F/gas mark 6.

Add the tomatoes to the courgette mixture and simmer away until all the vegetables are well cooked and soft and the tomatoes have reduced down to a thick rich tomato sauce.

Transfer to an ovenproof dish. Top with the grated cheese and bake in the oven until the cheese is melted, bubbling and gently browning at the edges.

Chicken with roasted fennel and puttanesca butter

This is a relatively simple dish, but has a real luxuriousness to it. Loaded with good fats, low GL and intense flavour combinations.

SERVES 1

1 skin-on chicken breast
1 small fennel bulb, sliced lengthways
sea salt and freshly ground black pepper
1 tbsp unsalted butter
5 anchovy fillets, chopped
2 tsp black olives, sliced
1 tsp capers, drained and rinsed

Preheat the oven to 200°C/400°F/gas mark 6.

Place the chicken breast and fennel on a baking tray, season with salt and pepper and bake for around 25 minutes. Turn the fennel occasionally to ensure some of the fat from the chicken coats it during roasting.

In a small pan, melt the butter and add the anchovies, olives and capers.

Plate the fennel up first in a small pile in the centre of a plate. Top with the chicken breast, then smother with the butter.

Beetroot, Puy lentil and goat's cheese warm salad

I know the word 'salad' doesn't make you think of a filling dinner. But this is an exception to that rule. Seriously filling, masses of B vitamins, very low GI, earthy and creamy.

SERVES 2

200g Puy lentils
2 raw beetroot, cut into wedges, skin left on
2 tbsp olive oil, plus more for the beetroot
2 tsp balsamic vinegar
sea salt and freshly ground black pepper
110g bag mixed baby leaf salad
150g goat's cheese

Place the lentils in a pan and cover with boiling water. Simmer until the lentils are tender. Preheat the oven to 200°C/400°F/gas mark 6.

Place the beetroot wedges on a baking sheet, drizzle with a little olive oil and roast at the top of the hot oven for around 25 minutes, until softening. Turn occasionally.

Mix the 2 tbsp of olive oil and the balsamic vinegar together, along with a little salt and pepper, then whisk well to create a dressing.

Assemble the salad by tossing the baby leaves and cooked, drained lentils together, then divide into two portions.

Place the beetroot wedges on top, crumble over the goat's cheese and drizzle over the dressing.

Tuna sweet potato fishcakes

I have my good friend Catherine Tyldesley to thank for the inspiration for this recipe. I have made many versions, but this simple one is the best. This makes quite a few fishcakes so you might have some left for breakfast, too, when they would be great with a poached egg on top.

SERVES 2

2 medium sweet potatoes, peeled and chopped
150g canned tuna (I prefer 'no drain')
2 tsp chopped coriander leaves
1 small red onion, finely chopped
½ tsp English mustard
1 egg, lightly beaten
1–2 tsp olive oil

Boil the sweet potatoes for about 15 minutes, or until soft and mashable, then drain.

Transfer the sweet potatoes to a bowl and mash them well. Add the tuna, coriander, onion, mustard and egg. Mix well.

Shape into cakes and gently fry in the olive oil until golden brown on each side.

Serve with a side salad, or cooked quinoa.

Baked salmon with rosemary white beans and buttered spinach

Simple and satisfying, this brings together virtually every essential nutrient for the health of the nervous system.

SERVES 1

1 salmon fillet
2 garlic cloves,
    finely chopped
2 tsp olive oil
sea salt
200g canned cannellini
    beans, drained
1 sprig of rosemary
200g baby spinach
2 tsp butter

Preheat the oven to 200°C/400°F/gas mark 6.

Place the salmon on a baking tray and bake for around 15 minutes.

Meanwhile, sauté the garlic in the olive oil, along with a good pinch of sea salt, for around three minutes. Add the beans and the rosemary with 1 tbsp of water and simmer and stir for about 10 minutes. Discard the rosemary sprig, as its flavour will have infused by now.

Quickly sauté the spinach in the butter just long enough for the leaves to wilt.

Make a bed of spinach on a plate and add the rosemary-flavoured beans. Place the salmon on top and serve.

Chocolate-coated energy bars

Now that you know that you need lots of magnesium to support your nervous system, you will be elated to know that chocolate – good-quality of course – is an incredibly rich source of magnesium. There is a god!!

MAKES 6

8 tbsp mixed seeds (flax, pumpkin, sesame, sunflower and so on)
3 handfuls of goji berries
handful of pitted dates
4 tbsp cocoa powder
1 tsp desiccated coconut
200g 70–80 per cent cocoa solids chocolate
3 tbsp coconut oil

Place all the ingredients, except the chocolate and coconut oil, into a food processor, and pulse a few times to create a stiff, coarse paste.

Spoon the coconut oil into a glass bowl, then sit the glass bowl in some freshly boiled water. In a matter of seconds the oil will melt. Add the melted oil to the food processor, then process the ingredients on high power until all have thoroughly mixed into a smooth firm paste.

Line a small cake tin or flan dish (about 25cm in diameter) with cling film, scrape in the paste and press down firmly to completely fill it.

Break the chocolate into small pieces into a heatproof bowl. Set over a pan of boiled water (taken off the heat) and melt slowly. Drizzle the melted chocolate over the top of the paste.

Place in the fridge for three hours, until set firm. Slice into about six even pieces (double quantity shown here).

Curry cashews These are an awesome mineral-packed low GI snack. You can't eat just one.

MAKES 6 SERVINGS
200g raw cashew nuts
1 tsp runny honey
½ tsp curry powder
pinch of salt

Preheat the oven to 170°C/340°F/gas mark 3½.

Place the cashew nuts into a bowl and drizzle over the honey. Toss the cashews well to ensure they are evenly coated.

Sprinkle over the curry powder and toss well again to make sure the cashews are all coated with curry powder.

Place the coated cashews on a baking tray lined with greaseproof paper, place at the top of the oven and bake for 10–12 minutes until beginning to turn golden.

Cool on the tray, sprinkle with salt, then transfer the nuts to an airtight container to store. If they last that long...

Two-herb houmous I am a bit of a houmous addict, I have to be honest. I like to jazz it up a little, too. Adding herbs brings another dimension to this already tasty dip.

MAKES 4–6 SERVINGS
400g can of chickpeas,
    drained and rinsed
1 large garlic clove,
    finely chopped
juice of ½ lemon
1 tbsp tahini
leaves from a small
    bunch of basil,
    roughly chopped, plus
    more to serve (optional)
leaves from a small
    bunch of parsley,
    roughly chopped
2–3 tbsp olive oil

Place all the ingredients into a blender or food processor and process into a smooth dip.

Sprinkle with a few tiny basil leaves, if you like, then serve.

Green smoothie Green smoothies often put people off because of their colour and the fact that they contain so much vegetation. With the addition of fruit and a vanilla protein powder, the 'green flavour' just vanishes. What better way to get more greens into your diet?

MAKES 1
250ml apple juice
1 ripe banana, broken
   into small pieces
4 handfuls of
   baby spinach
1 heaped scoop of vanilla
   whey protein powder

Place all the ingredients into a blender and blend into a smooth drink.

Chocolate crunch pots A lovely rich chocolatey dessert, with a secret ingredient.

SERVES 2
2 very ripe (make sure they are soft to the touch) avocados
3 tbsp cocoa powder
3-4 tsp honey
1 tbsp coconut oil
6 oat cakes

Scoop the flesh of the avocados into a blender or food processor. Add the cocoa powder and honey. Place the coconut oil in a heatproof bowl, then sit the bowl in some freshly boiled water. In a matter of seconds the oil will melt. Add the melted oil to the food processor. Process into a smooth chocolate mousse-like mixture.

Crumble the oat cakes and divide between two glass tumblers. Spoon the chocolate mixture over the top. Place in the fridge and chill for two or three hours.

Berry crumble This is super-charged with huge amounts of flavonoids and gives you that perfect balance between naughty and nice!

SERVES 2
200g blueberries
200g blackberries
porridge oats (see recipe
    method for amount)
2 tbsp ground flax seeds
1 tsp ground cinnamon

Place the blueberries and blackberries into a saucepan with 2 tbsp of water. Simmer over a medium-high heat for 30–40 minutes. This constant simmering will let the fruit break down and begin to take on a jam-like texture, without the need to add thickeners. Preheat the oven to 200°C/400°F/gas mark 6.

Transfer the fruit to a medium-small ovenproof dish. Now, here's why there was no set weight for the oats. You need to do this by eye. Top with enough oats to give you an even topping of about 5mm thick! Baking dishes vary so much, this is the easiest way to get it even.

Sprinkle over the flax seeds and cinnamon and place at the top of the oven for 10–12 minutes, until the crumble topping begins to get crunchy and turns a little golden.

INDEX

Clare Hulton – we are really cooking on gas now! Amazing work. Thank you! Jenny Liddle – you are tireless at what you do! Tanya Murkett – as always, supporting me and putting up with me no matter what! A big thank you to all the team at Quadrille, Smith & Gilmour, Martin Poole and Aya Nishimura. Catherine Tyldesley, Gaby Roslin and all of the wonderful people that have supported my work and career. Ramsay and Candy. Mum and Dad.

Editorial director: Anne Furniss
Creative director: Helen Lewis
Project editor: Lucy Bannell
Art direction and design: Smith & Gilmour
Photography: Martin Poole
Illustration: Blindsalida
Food stylist: Aya Nishimura
Props stylists: Polly Webb-Wilson & Wei Tang
Production: Tom Moore

First published in 2015 by Quadrille Publishing Limited

www.quadrille.co.uk

Cataloguing in Publication Data: a catalogue record for this book is available from the British Library.

978 184949 544 8

Printed in China